Walking Sticks

Walking Sticks

poems

by

Dudley Laufman

Illustrated by Jacqueline Laufman

Beech River Books

Center Ossipee, N.H.

Copyright © 2007 by Dudley Laufman

BⓇB

Beech River Books
P.O. Box 62, Center Ossipee, N.H. 03814
1-603-539-3537
www.beechriverbooks.com

LIBRARY OF CONGRESS CATALOGING-IN-PUBLICATION DATA

Laufman, Dudley.
Walking sticks : poems / by Dudley Laufman ; illustrated
by Jacqueline Laufman. -- 1st ed.
p. cm.
ISBN-13: 978-0-9793778-2-2 (pbk. : alk. paper)
ISBN-10: 0-9793778-2-X (pbk. : alk. paper)
1. New England--Poetry. I. Title.
PS3562.A79W35 2007
811'.6--dc22
2007011461

Printed in the United States of America

To Jacqueline.

ACKNOWLEDGEMENTS

Some of these poems will have appeared in the following magazines, journals and anthologies: *Echoes, Bee Culture, Hanging Loose, Rivendell, Abbeywood, Plainsong, South Boston Literary Gazette, Plain Brown Wrapper, Yasou, American Weave, The Oak, Union, Northwoods Anthology, Wind In The Timothy Press.com, Wind In The Timothy Broadsides, Centripetal, Red Owl, The Sow's Ear, New Hampshire Times, Hard Row To Hoe, Off The Coast; Waterways, Skyline, Country Dance & Song, Baby Clam, Touchstone, Canterbury Newsletter, Fight Those Bastards, Sahara, Spitball, Color Wheel, Pine Island Journal, Love's Chance, Sweet Annie, Animus, Other Side of Sorrow, GreenPrints, Prose Poem Anthology, Aesops's Feast, Prairie Schooner, Open Spaces 1, ASTA, Origin at Longhouse,* and in the following collections: I HEAR RINGING REELS, WIND IN THE TIMOTHY, WEE HERD'S WHISTLE, DANCING MASTER'S DIARY, OF THE FERN, ORCHARD & GARDEN, MOUTH MUSIC, HOW CONTRA DANCING WAS INVENTED, SMOKE SCREEN, BULL.

Broadsides: HOW TO BECOME A SWAN, GAME, AND GOING FOR A WALK printed letterpress by Canterbury Shaker Villag; THE CALENDAR ACCORDING TO DUDLEY by Golgonooza Letter Foundry & Press, (Dan Carr, Ashuelot, N.H.); GIVEN by Bull Thistle Press, Jamacia, VT. (Greg Joly); COW BELLS in the Longhouse Card Series (Bob Arnold).

Other books and chapbooks by Dudley Laufman

I HEAR RINGING REELS. (Wind in the Timothy Press, 1962).

THE WOLFHUNTERS. (Self, 1964).

BEG OF FOXES. (Gibson's Book Store, 1966).

WIND IN THE TIMOTHY. (Self, 1965).

WEE HERD'S WHISTLE. (Vermont Stoveside Press, 1967).

OF THE FERN. (Self, 1973).

ORCHARD & A GARDEN. (William Bauhan Press, 1974).

A DANCING MASTER'S DIARY. (Self, 1981).

THE MAGIC POCHETTE. (Self, 1981).

MOUTH MUSIC. (Wind in the Timothy Press, 2001).

HOW CONTRA-DANCING WAS INVENTED. (Wind in the Timothy Press, 2002).

I WAS A FIDDLER BEFORE I CAME HERE. (Self, 2002).

BULL. (Wind in the Timothy Press, 2003).

SMOKE SCREEN. (A Pudding House Chapbook, 2004).

THE STONE MAN. (Canterbury Shaker Village, 2005).

For CDs and other works by Dudley Laufman, please visit the website: *www.laufman.or*g.

CONTENTS

I. UP THE LAKE

II. MOUTH MUSIC

III. NARRATIVE

IV. TRANSLATIONS

V. WEE HERD'S WHISTLE

VI.   A GLASS OF SCRUMPY

VII.   ON THE EDGE OF THE BURREN

VIII. LOVE POEMS

I.

Up the Lake

SEA BURIAL

This old merchant mariner
desired a sea burial
Scatter my ashes on the sea
he said having moved inland
His church oversaw it
My mom was on the committee
She says to one of the other members
We have a job to do
and he says
I took care of it
She asks *Where*
hoping of course for
someplace coast of Maine
maybe Ordiorne Pont
or at least Nahant
City Point he says
and all Mom can think of is
oil refineries and dumps
She asks *When*
He says *Yesterday*
St. Patricks Day
and she thinks Lord
all those Irish and green beer

Years later I get into Southie
see all those old three-deckers
with wonderful oak doorways

look out into the harbor
through those islands
all the way to Spain
If Mom were alive
(she had her ashes scattered
on Lake Winnepausaukee
all those summer folks)
I would say to her
It's ok Mom
Southie is ok

DOIN' DONUTS

In February we went
out on the frozen lake
in a Model A pickup

A slight touch to the brake
and around we went
around and around
in dizzying vortices
across the ice
all the way to Melvin Village

Went ashore to Ralph Piper's house
a white cape with black shutters
In the kitchen the shiny
black wood burning stove
warmed the room
Sunlight shafts on the table
where we drank strong coffee
ate hot crisp donuts

THE SWIM

Waiting patiently for the time
watching the dew dry on the nasturtiums

Down the hill to the pond
tomatoes growing
on the narrow strip of ground
between the sidewalk and the gutter

Down the granite steps
into the pond

Moms sat on the stone steps
knitting visiting watching us
None of us could swim
Don't go out over your head
   they kept saying

The pond smelled brackish
It was connected to a
smaller pond across Route 2
The little pond
drained into the Alewife
which fell to the Mystic
which was tidal
Gave us a tie to the sea

I played with a lopsided
wooden boat I had made

Unattended she
headed out to sea

I lunged for it
turned for shore but
couldn't touch bottom
The boat wouldn't hold me up
Water over my nose ears
Could see my mom
put down her knitting
I felt weeds then muck
then good old sand

A rush of sound
traffic starting up over on Route 2

I spent the rest of the time
sitting in an inch of water
on the sand by the steps
beaching my boat again and again

Towel over shoulders
walked up the hill barefoot
pavement still warm
smells of supper
evening spicy nicotiana

UP THE LAKE

They come up from Melrose Winchester
places like that near Boston
Have a big cottage on the lake
Chris Craft boat water skiis
float dock barbeque everything

Loan the place out to friends relatives
come up onna weekends
Going up the lake they say
Have it to themselves in August
Wear shorts no shoes
Canoe to hidden coves and islands
find wild blueberries
After supper cards by the
soft light of kerosene lamps
Sleep on the porch
hearing the water lap the
white sand shore
Go home after Labor day

The boy is sad
hates to leave
Says When I grow up
I'm gonna live here alla time

They come up good weather weekends
last time in October

pull the boat
put it up
beach the float and the dock
shut off the water
drain the pipes

There's a nip to the air
too cold to swim
Close up the house

Settle in at school jobs
football and track
pumpkins burning leaves

By November the cottage too has
settled in for winter
The dark pines gather in
Probably has snowed once
Woodsmoke from a nearby year rounder
The lake is glass ready to freeze

The family never comes up in winter
but if the boy could
wouldn't he just love it

HOME RUN

The ball field of my back yard
was a mixture of Fenway Park and Ebbets Field
Both teams played there
in cross league action
This was before such scheduling occurred
but I was ahead of the times

The arborvitea hedge was the
left field green monster
the house (white) was center field
the garage was the concave
right field wall of Ebbets
that Duke Snider used to
play the rebounds with his back to home
The fence between it and the house
was the bull pen
Home was under the pink Judas tree
the back stop was the compost pile
The clothesline guarded the bullpen
if one landed there it was an out

I was the designated hitter
for both teams for all the batters
Again ahead of the times
never ran the bases
I was Ted Williams   Joe Cronin
Johnny Pesky   Bobby Doer

Jim Tabor   Johnny Pitlak
Birdie Tibbets   Mel Ott
Dom DiMaggio   Joe Dobson
With my little souvenier bat and golf balls
(which I got from caddying for my father
evenings at the Arlmont)
I hit home runs over the monster hedge
out onto Landsdowne St (Rt 60 and Pleasant)
doubles off the center field wall
never broke a window
inside the parkers to tricky right center
where the mint and chamomile grew
Would run out of pellets
every three innings or so
have to go retrieve them on the street
or risk scratches in the roses
I never got them all
Now years later
one could find a ball or two
buried in the mulch
under the green monster

When we got rained out
went to another park in the cellar
The game was broadcast by tickertape
The park a mixture of
Braves Field and Polo Grounds

was set up on the ping-pong table
A green erector set metal box
was the left field wall
slanting to deep center
I used an even smaller miniature bat
and marbles for missiles
They would echo off the wall
for doubles or even triples
Like that game at Fenway
when Arlington met the hicks
from Shelburne Falls Mass
for the state title
Arlington led 4-1 top of the 9th
Mel Massuco weakening pitcher
allowed those farm boys from the Berkshires
to put them off the wall
with a resounding boom
each one spelling doom
and Arlington lost 5-4

My favorite games were after supper
Could smell the new cut lawn
I had mowed that afternoon
Could smell Gus Porter's cigar next door
I had just pounded three homers in a row
over the green monster
and I ran into the house to tell my father

He was in the bedroom
sitting in the black rocking chair
and reading the BOSTON EVENING TRANSCRIPT
He said, *When you can do that for real*
when I can read about it here
then you can jump up and down

Got sent down to the minors
then took up dairy farming
Like many gum chewing coaches
Daddy had a hard time
telling me he loved me

FIRE STATION

The eight-sided fire station
in Arlington Centre
has eight doors
with a red engine
behind each door
ready to go the way it points
ready to roar like
Menotomy Minutemen

The firemen live upstairs
waiting for the bell to send them
spinning down the brass pole
onto the rumbling truck

A bear hugging firefighter
took me
        eight years old
teeth gritting
        heart in mouth down the pole

Truck smelled of new red paint

FIRST KISS

was with
tom boy Jean Dorian
coming home
from a football game

Early fall
smell of leaves burning
walking along
side by side

I wanted to
take her hand
but was afraid to
so rested it
on her shoulder
and she dragged us along

Time to go   our own streets
the gang gathers around
Kiss her   Kiss her
shout Sally and Clark
Teddy and Paula
Ooh says Jean
on the mouth

Lips and teeth

CHAINS

Back in the Thirties
they had those
chain driven Mack trucks
with a big M
curving down the front of the radiator grill
and the indented sides of the hood
The trucks went zig zig zig
along Pleasant Street

To gain our hill after a snow storm
we had to put on chains
either a full set which
you laid the out on the packed snow
backed over them
brought them up around the tire
hooked them up
or used those strap on kind

Backed down the hill to a flat place
got a running start
kept it up til you made it
Not much traffic in those days
Snow stayed packed on the roads
but chains still broke
could hear them clacking along
into the white emptiness of night

Horse drawn wooden plows
did the sidewalks
bumping along the broken pavement
ravaged and bruised from tree roots
heaved up by falling trees
'38 hurricane

Hear them coming
grinding by
at three in the morning
horses snorting
heavy chains swaying
from harness to whiffletree

TWILIGHT LEAGUE

We'd go down the game
summertime
Waltham vs
Spy Pond Nine

No fence around the park
deep left had the
B & M railroad track
Boys Club was at deepest center
edge of the pond
No one broke any windows
Tennis court way out right
had a fence
trucks and cars parked
but nobody could hit that far

So the 6:15
Boston to Lexington
comes chugging along
and Tucker hits one
across the tracks
front of the engine

Waltham left fielder
scoots thru the underpass
returns waving the ball
but Tucker is home
standing up

Ground rule double
yell the Waltham bench

Ground rule triple
says cigar smoking
straw hatted Spy Ponders

Home run says the ump
as the train rumbles off to Lexington
like Paul Revere
and we could hear the echo
from the tennis court
like in that film BLOW UP
hear a dog bark
in the oncoming dark

BLUE COAT, RED COAT

April 19, On The Road To Boston

Never played cowboys 'n Indians
cops 'n robbers just did
blue coat red coat
especially mid April

At noontime would watch
William Dawes and Paul Revere
gallop up Mass Ave to the town hall
get off (Paul usually fell off)
go inside pee cuppa coffee
laced with rum
mount and gallop off to Lexington

Then we'd go into town
to Exeter Street
see the marathon finish
then to Braves Field
watch the opener

Back out in Menotomy
late afternoon
play blue coat red coat
Us underdog little kids
had to be the
big dog lobsterbacks
March down the street
older bigger kids

were the good guys
hiding behind trees
bang bang you're dead
had to fall down in the
still winter wet leaves
count to sixty
get up march again
follow the fight
through the neighborhood
call them cowards
come out and fight
like it said in our history books

Sometimes they let us
be the minutemen
The underdog underdogs
Won't fall down
when we shoot them
say we are cowards
ride up behind us
clippity clop bang bang
you're dead
Shoe is on the other foot

What if I had
been alive back in 1775
Have a farm in West Cambridge

edge of the Mystic River
Left the family behind
hiding in the woods
Brought up a Quaker
carry my musket
(used for hunting only)
Get behind a tree
see the redcoats coming
down the road towards us
tall resplendent in their uniforms
stopping to load and fire
My neighbor George falls
I pee my britches

HOW LAUFMAN CAME TO AMERIKA

My father always said we came from Switzerland
that we were Swiss
Laufman is a Swiss name he said
This was back in 1942 when
being German wasn't popular

But anyway we know
his name was Philip
born April 6 1767
somewhere in Hessen Germany
like maybe Bad Zwesten
near the River Weser
Might have been on a farm
right in the village
dwelling up over the stable
getting some heat
rising up from the cattle below
great big tile stove
Father was a farmer or logger
tavern keeper maybe
or captained the ferry

Philip was a Hessian soldier
Sixteen years old
Recruited one way or another
to fight as an auxiliary
for the Brits against the rabble in America
or even *for* the colonists *against* the Brits

(John Adams was considering this
Wouldn't that have been a scene)
Guess that didn't happen
Don't know if he was pressed into service
or made drunken
woke up on the boat
Possibly he was bribed
or his father sold him
Could have joined of his own free will
to escape poverty of Germany
or for adventure
Maybe to leave a pregnant frauline

He served as a drummer boy
Probably couldn't see well enuff to shoot
blind in one eye like me

Upon arrival in America
he deserted
in the dark of night
joined American troops
He was at Yorktown when the
Lord Cornwallis Fife & Drum played
THE WORLD TURNED UPSIDE DOWN

Took his pay tax free
and set up as tavern keeper

in the Hessen like hills of Pennsylvania
where he made good German beer

He married one Mary Pence
had a passel of children
one of whom was Jacob
German accents gone by this time
Jacob married Margaret Keefer
had a brood of youngsters
while farming in Illinois
A son Keefer married Harriet Shively
and they had William my Grampa
who was a millwright and fiddler
His third wife bore my daddy Miller
who married Marjorie Dick from Boston
and from that union
in comes I like it or like it not
let's hope that Dudley will never be forgot

HURRICANE

Trees toss violently
tipping my window to a
precarious angle

Salt spray and seagull feathers
snap against the pane
even though we are
seven miles inland

By propping myself
on my elbow
and humming Brahm's VARIATIONS
ON A THEME BY HAYDEN
I am able to abate the storm

IN WINTER

In winter
the slates on our roof
slope down to the shore

giving a good start
to skate downwind

I am a glass cutter
marking curious goldfish
prehistoric whalebones

On warm days
there is the smell
of celery

SALISBURY

Morning of Christmas Eve
I'm emailing friend John
in Salisbury England
asking Do you guys
go to the Haunch of Venison
have a glass of
hot whiskey and cinnamon
walk the dark streets after
to yer own wall
Or before that do you get to
listen to Christmas music
in the cathedral
that massive organ
Oh how wondrous if you do

And he replies
Yes indeed
we do have the odd pint
at the Haunch
sing Drive Dull Cares Away
trod the narrow lanes home
cuppa chamomile laced with rum
before bed
We've never yet
been to midnight mass
in the cathedral
but as Carol's dad is
staying with us and he is
very fond of carols
it's just possible
we could be
heading for that north door
in about two hours time

II.

Mouth Music

THE BAMPTON BRIGADOON

Spring Bank Holiday - every year

Them lucky lads of the Bampton Morris
some of em scarcely
more'n twelve years old
start their day with HIGHLAND MARY
dance all day long
trudging by sunset
their bells almost to their ankles

One of them watches the fiddler
who plays just like the Jinky
ruff and a bit flat
and you know the lad
wants to do it
exactly the same way
you can tell by the way he looks

So they sit there
at the Romany Inn
it's getting on towards midnight
(one of em has already gone home)
waiting to dance the
last one of the day and year
which will be HIGHLAND MARY
to THE QUAKER
wondering how they will
pass the time til next year

THE MAGIC POCHETTE
A Ladle Fadle

> *One day he made a little violin*
> *A little fiddlekin*
> *That could play all by itself.*
>
> German folk song
> Sung by Richard Dyer Bennett

Having taken up cigars he accumulated boxes of all shapes and sizes. One day he made a liddle fiddle from a small narrow box. It fit in his coat pocket so he called it Pochette. Every time he played her, he found a new cigar inside.

One morning he heard a familiar merry tune. Pochette had sprouted legs by her tuning pegs and was playing herself and dancing around. *Wow* he said.

He took his act to Boston Common. They had fun playing and making lots of money from the passerby. And lots of cigars.

He bought a harmonica so he could play duets with Pochette. She said *Ouch* when he tightened her pegs up to pitch. When he wasn't looking she played the harmonica. He got a rig and played Pochette and the harmonica at the same time. While he smoked, Pochette put on the rig and played the harmonica and herself together.

Next day he bought a tin whistle. While counting the money she played the whistle. He played a pipe and tabor. So did Pochette.

He was upset. *She can play everything I can play, and better.* A standerby said, *Imitation is the highest form of compliment.*

Yeah, but I can't make cigars.

True, but you can smoke them.

COME ALONG YOU LUCKY LADS, COME ALONG

Bampton in the Bush,
Oxfordshire, England, Whit Monday 2004

> *O dancing is a great thing,*
> *A great thing to me!*
> — Thomas Hardy

You wonder how it must be
for old athletes like Johnny Pesky
Joe Cronin   Ted Williams
Maurice Richard   Woody Dumart
to have to retire their bats
hang up their skates
Must be the same for musicians
or old morris dancers
but these guys they
still go to the games concerts
or street shows
most of them anyway
For some it must be tough
In Bampton England for instance
there's old Francis Shergold
brown wrinkled
in full Bampton Morris kit
pint of bitter in hand
watches his side dance THE WEBBLY
outside the Horse Shoe Inn

His younger brother Roy
like a walnut
best dancing fool
Bampton ever had
passes by on the
other side of street
hoe on shoulder
on his way to
dig in someone's orchard
barely waves

Francis saying
Look at them lucky lads
Aren't they having a good time

I used to dance like that
wish I could now
can't get the
old knees up can I

Francis thinking
I'll have another pint
then go home
sit in the garden

ARAN STEAMER

There is no noise
Silence is the only sound

When the Aran steamer
glides to the pier
at Galway City
gulls whirl in the gray sky

David Curry's Orchestra
plays SHANDON BELLS JIG
from a radio on the bridge

Rooks punctuate chimney pots

Passengers slip away
like a fan

FIDDLEHEAD FERN

Which came first,
the fern or the fiddle

Must have been the fiddle
poking up out of the ground
in a woodsy place No

The fern came first and they
called it a fiddlehead   No

If they made the scroll on the fiddle
why didn't they call it
a fern head fiddle

No The fern came first
growing out there all alone
no name all those years
then someone scrolled
the head of a fiddle
and the fern gets a name

Ever eat them
the fern not the fiddle
although it must look like the fiddler
is going to eat the thing butt first

Not I I hold the fiddle on my chest
play from my heart.

DANCING IN COUNTY CLARE

It is Sunday night

The pub is shaped
like a horseshoe magnet

A fiddle and concertina
play at one end
their music rough
like the broken end
of a whetstone

A dance is in progress
where the current
moves both ways

The girls are mini-skirted
white as gulls

The men are in church clothes
dark as ravens

They rise glide and dip
slanting in slapping
their feet on the cement
like surf under the
cliffs at Dereen

FIRST CHANGE

Only three miles away tonight
Near enough to ride horseback
Started off normally enough
five toes on each foot etc
riding over high plains
sage smelling juniper
then slanting off into
humus and leaf mold

My horse said
Most guys come to a hill
they trots up
but not me man
I'll walk up easy like

I knew then I was beginning
to think like a horse
And when I swished my pony tail
to brush away deer flies
I knew the change was complete

We arrived late
strands of sweet fern
stuck in our hooves
whinnying trumpets of heat lightning.

GRAMPS

Used to be a fiddler in Illinois
shot up a dance once
it being on the dull side
spent the night in jail

Anyway here he is now years later
living in a retirement home
Walks up to the local dance
straw hat yellow shirt
blue tie white pants cane
to the teeth as he used to say
Went and sat by the band

The caller was a young feller
dressed sort of like the old scratch
you'd think they was related

Girl comes in
thin willow of a thing
dark hair pretty's all get out
see her slip through her dress
runs right up to the caller
throws her arms around the boy
cocks her leg up in back big kiss

Another girl more a woman
big busted long yellow hair

same scene
And one more
perhaps more plain but a honey
you can bet
same drill

The old man reaches out with his cane
taps the boy on the bum says
Hey   know what I would do I was you
I'd go home right now
while I was still ahead

I AM RAFTERY

(Transcription of a translation (Hyde)
of a Gaelic poem by Anthony Raftery)

I am Raftery the fiddler
The wandering bard
My eyes have no sight
But light is my heart

Going west on my journey
By the light of my soul
So tired and weary
To the end of my road

I've long spindly legs
And a shock of red hair
A way with the women
And with whiskey I fear

I wander the roads
Through Galway I go
All searching for love
On my way to Mayo

Behold me now
With my back to a wall
Playing music
For an empty hall.

MELLIE DUNHAM'S FIDDLE

was on display in Norway Maine
Some of us guys was standing around
waiting for a chance to give it a try
I was first
Barely had I touched it
and I had to kick off some snowshoes
The fiddle was like a dark
short-haired cat curled in my arms
purring waiting to be petted
I felt myself getting shorter stouter
Some tourist came by said
Hey play MELANCHOLY BABY man
Alright says I *but it is going to sound*
a hell of a lot like POP GOES THE WEASEL

I yelled out *Let 'er rip* (I never do that)
and played RORY O'MORE in the key of G
major all the way raspy old tune
Some old ladies sitting there said
Doesn't he sound just like old Mellie

I pushed back my mop of white hair
tweaked my handlebar moustache
handed the fiddle to Greg and said
Do HULL'S VICTORY
Joined him on my fiddle
Didn't see what he did with his snowshoes

There was no handlebar let alone a walrus
Greg never saws but there he was
going at it furiously saying
You never play in F

I'm not I say
Yes you are says he

No suh I'm on D the way Mellie played it
How you like my moustache

You don't have a moustache says Greg

Sure do just like Mellie's

Lord says Greg *moustache and HULL'S on D*
what did you have to drink
as he handed the fiddle to Dave
who looks like Mellie anyway
moustache and all
so we couldn't tell
if the magic worked with him
as he played TURKEY IN THE STRAW

MOUTH MUSIC

Lived on a farm he did
up Cape Breton way
back from the sea a bit
but with tide
Said they dragged the river
bottom each spring to bring
up the sludge you know
for to spread on the fields

Did you go to the square dances I says
Oh sure says he *and many's the time
I tuned up a dance too*

Tuned up a dance says I
*what do you mean by that
you went around and tuned
up the fiddles*

Hell no he says *I tuned up the dance
We hummed the tunes don't ye know
mouth music we called it
Some call it lilting
Here's MISS MCLEODS REEL
Deedle di de didle di dum deedle dum
see now how it goes
We used to dance out on
the weather gray wharf in the salty inlet*

spruces by the rocky shore
gulls above wheeling and mewing
Four old men with white beards
sat in the first row
they were the first rate tuners
One of them always held my sister on his knee
We younger chaps
stood in the second row
being second-raters

I'll tell ye there's a power of music
in the tongue makes toes itch

ON THE WAY HOME

a deer leaped across the road
with a woman astride
wearing pale green see through
And wings.
I wish she would stop
sit in the car with me
I have coffee in a thermos
We would have to do
something about the wings
Perhaps they fold up

What about her deer
She could tie it to a tree
That would never work
have you ever seen a deer tied up
She could let it go
catch another one
they go by all the time—every ten minutes

I'm sure we could
solve the problem of the wings

THE SWEETS OF MAY

The spice of the currant blossom
floats upon the air
makes my feet go up and down
a garland in my hair

For I am a country dancer
the best you've ever seen
Golden is my partner
with a smock of green

We dance around the lilacs
and through the greeny grass
as the music slides and trembles
and the May lasts

on into the summer
June and then July
autumn and longy winter
all the seasons die

O how I love the springtime
and the May again
when the men dance around the ladies
and the ladies go round the men

WOOD

This is the log
that comes from a tree
that is felled to the ground
that is hauled to the mill
and sawed into boards
that makes the fiddle
that makes the music
that makes feet thump
the floor that is made of wood

This is the sheep
who gives of her wool
and this is the fleece
that lines the case
where lies the fiddle
that is made of wood
And this selfsame sheep
has the guts that cross the bridge
to bring out music
that lies in the wood

Here is the horse
who has the tail
that provides the hair
that spans the bow
that touches the gut
that makes the music
that comes from the wood

There is the tree
that secretes its sap
which then become rosin
to rub on the bow
which then grabs the strings
making them vibrate with music
that comes from the wood.

This is the hand
that draws the bow
across the strings
that sing of maple and spruce
and these are the fingers
that press the strings
against the ebony
for a night of dancing

And all the time
the feet are tapping
feet are thumping
all the time these feet are thumping
on the floor that is made of wood

III.

Narrative

I WAS A FIDDLER BEFORE I CAME HERE

Had a little farm on the hillside
above the village that was
only there four days a week
All rocks ponds mosquitoes
summer folks early frost
no place to do farming
Can't say I didn't try
Augmented my earnings
playing fiddle across in Maine
at that barn there
LADY OF THE LAKE to my favorite
tune HASTE TO THE WEDDIN'

Had a woman lived with me
but she didn't like winters
Left me to do for myself
Couldn't pay the taxes
lost the place
went to live with Sis
in Haverhill but she died
Wandered the roads
'til they took me to the Home
Missed my farm
The steam pipes talked
to me at night nasty stuff
I'd talk back throw things
Next thing I knew
was down here at the State

Sit on the ward
or out in the yard
think of my farm
or of playing fiddle

Man and woman come by
playing guitars singing
stuff like WILD IRISH ROSE
JINGLE BELLS and that sort
Brought a young feller one time
playing a beat up old violin
I says to him said
I don't suppose you can
play anything else 'sides
those goddamn songs
He played JACKET TRIMMED IN BLUE
LITTLE JUDY OFF SHE GOES
Rough just like me
I couldn't believe it
Asked him *SPEED THE PLOW*
He played it
How you know that he asked
I was a fiddler 'fore I came here
You still play he asked   *Some I says*
Still have a fiddle   Yup
Get it we'll do some chunes

Did them every time he came by
Had the folks here jigging
I liked to hear him do
CINCINNATI HORNPIPE
never could myself
But he hired me play for dances
Met some other old
white haired fiddlers like myself

Brought me to his place f'dinner
Named one of his kids after me
Took me up to my old farm one October
stole some big red Baldwins
for me and the boys

Came by yesterday my birthday
Brought me a jar of peanut butter
Told him I couldn't play no more
fingers stiff
Too weak
Doubt I'll be around when the leaves fall

Gave him my fiddle and my gold watch
Said *Bury me up at my old farm*
Hope it will be snowing
Make me a stone says
I Was A Fiddler 'fore I Came Here

THE STONE HOUSE FIDDLER

And the house beats like a heart with
dance music
Because our boys have grown
to the age when girls are their music.

—Robinson Jeffers
from OCTOBER WEEKEND

They had become interested in square dancing and the
schottische...

—Donnan Jeffers
from THE BUILDING OF TOR HOUSE

The wind-up victrola had broken beyond repair
electricity was not strung to the point yet
and the twins wanted to have a dance
Their mother could play some of the jigs
on her parlor organ but the twins
wanted a fiddle for the square dances
So a message was sent up the canyon
to Willy the fiddler saying please come to
Stone House Saturday evening next to play
for a dance we will pay you five dollars
with food and drink and pasture for your horse

Saturday next Willy rode his horse down
through the dark redwood forest from his
cabin on the ridge and along the
Coast Road to the stone house Always wondered

what it looks like inside   who these folks are

Hi I'm Willy Hope you don't mind I don't
know how to call square dances it only
occurred to me I didn't tell you before

That's ok said the twin Donald *I know*
how from listening to the records we have
C'mon in and meet mother and father

Inside was stone with pine paneling
Low ceiling Father the poet sat by the fire
It was very quiet except for the sound
of the distant surf on the rocks below
Mother busied herself tidying up last minute
and asking *How long have you played the violin*
Since I was a kid answered Will
Fifteen years old maybe sixteen

                        Did you
have lessons

            Oh no said Will *I used to*
watch my dad and uncle they played fiddles
at the dances up Palo Colorado
'bout half way up in the deep redwoods there
Someone built a platform between three great
trunks had a cabin there where they sold whiskey
All the ranchers and burners came with wives

and sweethearts to thump upon that floor
I don't remember there being a caller but they
danced polkas waltzes two steps and reels
Everyone whirled around in such great style
and those fiddles were so happy I just
loved it so Daddy bought a tin fiddle
from the catalog I taught myself
to play by watching him and my old uncle

Do you know any Irish tunes on your fiddle

Yes PIPE ON THE HOB and TELL HER I AM
Those are jigs Know one reel MCLEODS
and a bunch of old songs and tunes like
TURKEY IN THE STRAW probably ten
altogether small lot but it does me

Mother sat at the organ said *Do you know this*

Oh sure PUT YOUR LITTLE FOOT that makes eleven
She said *I call that PADDY CANTOR singing*
Paddy Cantor Paddy Cantor Paddy Cantor Eye ay

Sure enough says Willy *and there is a dance*
goes with it I'll show the gang tonight

The gang trooped in laughing George, the other

58

twin said *Hope you don't mind we invited*
Gardner the gardner to play harmonica and his
wife Cookie she's not a cook to whack the
tambourine add a little gelatin
and volume to the pie
                              Great says Willy
I know Gardner didn't know he did
harmonica that's great Besides the twins
there were four or five other healthy
looking young men and a passel of pretty
young ladies Soon the dance was on
Willy played COMING ROUND THE MOUNTAIN
and Donald sang the calls to a square dance
Then everyone lined up for a Virginia Reel
Willy played IRISH WASHERWOMAN
scratching it out in great style Then he switched
to PIPE ON THE HOB Donald was askance
for a second but then he carried on
Gardner's harmonica was only in G so as the
jig was on D he struggled some
Never heard that tune he said after the
dance was through and everyone clapped and yelled
Do us a one two three hop…a schottische

Don't know any says Willy
                              I do says Gardner
and he blew into the FLOP EARED MULE

Only one two three hop he knows said
Twin number one corner of his mouth

The girls danced with all the boys Mother
danced one with each of her twins Someone
tried to get the poet to dance but he
would not move from the hearth sat there
with a faint smile on his face said *No*
thank you my poems are dance enough

Let's go outside to cool off said twin
number one and they all flocked outdoors
Willy nursed a cup of honey beer
while visiting with Gardner A cool breeze
wafted through the open door bringing
salty air into the room The fire
was unattended the poet having vanished
Needed fuel and fanning Willy took
some paper from the kindling pile noticing
that one scrap of paper had some lines
of verse scribbled on it He read some rimed
couplets about Peace O'Farrell...the poet
was making words love words like he made
stone love stone Into the embers with it
for Willy was sure that was where the poet wished it
He added Madrona bark and the blaze took life

The dancers returned Willy took note that in the
outside dark they had paired off There was
an extra girl and she sat by the fire
with the poet who had stolen back
She was slimish a gardenia in her
red hair Now's the time for PUT YOUR LITTLE FOOT
thought Willy and he beckoned to the girl
saying *will you dance with me Red 'til I
learn your name*

                     Red is nice she replied
*but name is June June Ramsay and yes
I would love to dance with the fiddler*

*Alright everyone get a partner for the
PUT YER LITTLE FOOT* June snuggled right in the
crook of Willy's arm Ma struck up
PADDY CANTOR on the organ and the
rest followed as Willy and June
put-your-little-footed-it around the room
him saying *Aren't I the dancing master now*

Donald sang another square dance then
signaled for the last Ginger Ale
*TURKEY IN THE STRAW this time and no
changing tunes* said Donald Such stomping
and clapping you never saw or heard as they
reeled their way up and down the set

A fine red dust rose up and sifted down
a pale maroon mix in the rosin film
The organ wheezed the harmonica wavered
the tambourine boomed and the fiddle screeched
Willy got them into a big ring
He noticed that Red had somehow jimmied the poet
off his chair and into the big circle
Willy motioned Gardner and Cookie into the
middle with him and the dancers wheeled
around them while the organ tried to keep up
All into the middle and crowd up close
Willy shouted above the tumult and he
did not miss the sly wink from June

Then the organ droned out SKYE BOAT SONG
Willy waltzed with June playing as well
resting his fiddle on her neck

Goodbyes so longs the room empty and still
Mother went to get Willy's money
stopped cupped her ear said *There's rain*
coming yes hear it on the windows
You can't go out in this please stay the night

I have a blanket roll on the horse said Willy
I'll get it from the wet
                    You may sleep in the
stone tower there is a cot on the second floor

Sleep well stay for breakfast Great dance Love the
fiddle and the dances Here's a light

The surf the wind and rain kept Willy from
immediate slumber and was resounding enough
that he did not hear the door open below
Half asleep he became aware
of a presence beside the cot peeling
off wet garments June slipped in beside him

By dawn the weather had cleared on the cool side
Willy was glad he had a sweater as wind
whistled through the turret And Red was gone

The dancers were at the table laden with
homemade bread and jam fruit and eggs

Morning Fiddler great dance last night

Where is that red haired girl who was my partner

Oh she comes and goes all the time
Lives with some folks just down the road
probably ran home last night in the rain

THE SCHOONER

The walrus and the carpenter were walking close at hand
They wept like anything to see such quantities of sand

If seven maids with seven mops swept it for half a year
Do you suppose, the walrus said, that they could sweep it
*   clear*
I doubt it said the carpenter and shed a bitter tear

—Lewis Carroll
   from THE WALRUS AND THE CARPENTER

Like I was telling you
I was walking along
Lucy Vincent Beach
on the Vineyard there
and I sees this skeleton
of a wrecked boat
sticking out of the sand at low tide
About ninety feet long
most of it buried in the mud
I have my waders on
poke around there
you can just make out the name
BASILE up by the bowsprit

Next chance I get over to Edgartown
I go to the
County of Duke's County Historical Society
(not Duke's County but the
County of Duke's County

64

and don't forget it)
where I find
documented under Old Wrecks
"The good ship BASILE..."
out of Weymouth Nova Scotia
set sail for Haiti in 1913
with a cargo of lumber
a captain, mate cook
and a couple of deck hands
the plan being to
return with a load of salt

Unloading lumber proved
too much for the captain
and he succumbed to heart failure
Last thing he said
Take 'er home boys
They turned the flag upside down
and headed north
Didn't see a sail for eleven days
Came into thick fog off Massachusetts
ran aground on Martha's Vineyard
Said Hell with this
left her lay
caught the packet for Boston
took a train to Digby

So I get my neighbor 'n his 'dozer
he builds a cofferdam
seaside of the wreck
to hold off the tide
'n with a come along
pulls the timbers
free from their grave
to high dry sand
We number each 'n every
salvaged beam 'n board
timber 'n spar
with yellow chalk
haul them off to his shed
stacked so's to dry off

Then I does a little searching
finds the relatives of the crew
gets myself up to Digby
same way they did
boat from the Haven
train from Woods Hole
to Boston to Digby
Finds that family
shows them pictures of the wreck
they's so excited they can't eat
Then they come down to the
Vineyard see for themselves

I show 'em about where the boat
first ran aground on South Beach
and where it got washed to
after the '38 hurricane
Kind of emotional for those folks

So was thinking of re-building it
but probably too much of a dream
Many of the timbers have rotted
over the years
Most likely what I'll do
is I'll stack the timbers on a barge
tow it down to Digby
Let 'er finish her voyage home

ST. SAMUEL'S ISLAND

sets out there in the bay
quite a ways out
beyond sight of United States
They has only one road
runs east and west
probably eight miles altogether
village more or less in the middle
Sign at one end
on the bluff, 'n
shot full of bullet holes
reads End Of Road
Sign at the other end reads
Other End Of Road
also peppered with shot

Only two cars on island
Sam (he wan't no saint)
owned a beat up old chevy
Gerry (he wan't no saint neither)
owned a Model A
One time he come back from the US
left his beer on the ferry
He was half way down the island
when he remembered
Did a quick U-ie
headed back up island
fast as his little car would go

took the turn at Doc's on two wheels
rolling over out onto the lawn
where Doc was farting around
with his blueberries
Climbing out through a broken window
Gerry said *Help me right 'er up Doc*
got to catch that boat 'fore she leaves
get my beer

Yeah that's the island where they
had that man plays the melodeon
to do concerts for the school kids
Woman comes up to him
says *I just love that record of yours*
'n he says *That's where that other copy went*
me mum has one an' you got the other
they only printed the two you know

So theys only two cars out there
Sam's and Gerry's
Rest of the guys got boats.
Anyway don't know how they did it
but they had a head on collision
one night late mid-island
totaled both vehicles

SPREADING IT

Load of cow shit on the upper twenty
had a big John Deere
could hardly turn it around in the field
fact had to break down the stone opening
it was too narrow to fit through

We only got the one tractor
with front end loader
had to unhitch the spreader each time
to load it up
Anyhow I'm sideways on the hill
and a rock gets caught in the sprocket
So I'm under the spreader
hot day   horse flies biting
pry up the chain with a crow bar
reach in to get stone
chain snaps back   pinning my arm
pulling me up four inches off the ground
I'm hanging there thinking
what a way to die
mile from home in the woods
Minds me of the time
I'm sharpening a cutter blade
Old Harry on the tractor
impatient to get home for cocktails
his foot slips on the clutch
tractor moves   cutter bar slides

cuts off tip of my finger jesus
Or of that poem by Hayden Carruth
Guy's spreading shit
bear comes charging out of woods
guys suddenly spreading more than cow shit

Where wuz I   Oh yeah
under the manure spreader
arm caught in the sprocket chain
Well I fergot I had my other hand
on the crow bar
so I use it to pry up the chain
arm slides out with the stone
smooth as silk
or rather slick as shit in this case

FORTY YEARS AGO

a young man comes into a dance
asks can we play something Irish
We do him FINNEGAN'S WAKE
and MAGGIE IN THE WOOD
So he comes to a few more dances
then shows up on my doorstep one day
hands me some Irish LPs
and a walking stick
knows I'm a hiker
Says *I made this out of alder*
He had carved a harp into the head
painted some Irish symbols
a whale   a shamrock   an evil eye
all varnished over smooth

It became my everyday walking stick
Kept it in the car to use
when away from home
Wore off most of the art work
and the memory of who made it

Now forty years later
we're doing a gig in Merrimac
and this feller comes in on crutches
makes his way over to the stage
nods to me I nod to him
He says *Guess you don't know me*

nor me you if we passed on the street
You might not remember
I'm Bob Bixby from forty years ago
met you up to Moultonboro
gave you some Irish records
Gallowglass Celi Band and like that
and a walking stick
doubt if you still have that though

I says *Hang on a sec*
and I run out to the car
fetch the stick
hand it to him
He runs his hands over it
says *I can't believe you still have this*
you might want to get a rubber tip
at a hardware store someplace
put on the end here
keep it from splitting
last another forty years

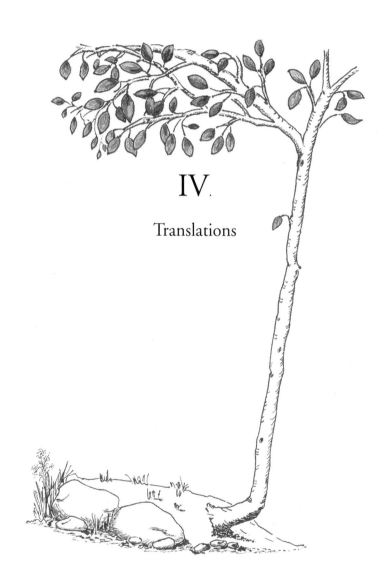

IV.

Translations

THE MADMAN †

A carolus or, better still
If you will, a lamb of gold.

—Manuscripts of the Kings's Library

The moon was combing her hair with an ebony comb,
silvering with a shower of gleaming sparks the hills, the fields,
and the woods.

Scarbo, the gnome who harvests hoards of gold, winnowed on
my roof to the creak of the weathercock - ducats and florins
dancing rhythmically, false coins littering the streets.

Thus laughed the madman who wanders every night through
the deserted city, one eye on the moon, the other—dead.

—Devil take the moon, he muttered, gathering up the devil's
tokens—I'll buy the pillory and warm myself there in the
sunlight.

But it was still the moon, the setting moon, and Scarbo,
wordless, in my cellar, coined ducats and florin, enough to tip
the scales.

And all the while, his horns outthrust, a snail lost in the night,
was seeking his way home on my lighted window panes.

---

† From GASPARD DE LA NUIT by Aloysius Bertrand
translated from the French by Dudley Laufman

SETTING OUT FOR THE NIGHTLY REVELS †

She got up at night, and, lighting the candle, took a bath,
and anointed herself, then, with several words, she was
transported to the nightly revels.

—Jean Bodin

(Of The Witches Deviltry)

A dozen of them were there, eating soup with beer, and for a spoon each of them had the forearm bone of a dead man.

The fireplace was red with coals, the candles mushroomed in the smoke, and the plates gave off the odor of a trench in springtime.

And when Maribas laughed or cried, one heard the moan of a bow on the three strings of a broken violin.

When the ruffians stretched out diabolically on the table, in the glimmer of the tallow, a burnt fly came to frolic on the black book.

This fly was still buzzing when, on his large and hairy stomach, a spider scaled the edges of the magic book.

But already sorcerers and witches had flown out the chimney, astride the broom, astride the tongs, and Maribas, on the handle of the frying pan.

---

† From GASPARD DE LA NUIT by Aloysius Bertrand
translated from the French by Dudley Laufman

MOONLIGHT †

Wake up, you sleepy heads
And pray for the dead.

—The cry of the night crier.

O, how sweet it is, when the bell shivers in the steeple at
night, to look at the moon with its face like a golden coin.

*
* *

Two lepers wept beneath my window, a dog howled at the
crossroads, and the cricket on my hearth prophesied softly.

But soon my ear caught only deep silence. The lepers were
home in their kennels, whipped home by the jailer who beats
his wife.

The dog had fled down a side street, before the pikes of the
watchman, rusted by the rain and pierced by the wind.

And the cricket had gone to sleep, as soon as the last scrap of
paper died gleaming in the fireplace ashes.

And it seemed to me—so confused is fever—that the moon,
grimacing, thrust out her tongue at me like a hanged man.

---

† From GASPARD DE LA NUIT by Aloysius Bertrand
translated from the French by Dudley Laufman

A DREAM †

I dreamed so much and more
but understood none of it.

—Pantagruel, Book III

It was night. At first there were—this I saw, this I tell—and
alley where the moon cracked through the walls, a forest
pierced by twisted paths—and Gallows Hill, swarming with
cloaks and hats.

Next there were—this I heard, this I tell—the death knell of a
bell answered by death cries from a dungeon—sad cries and
feral laughter, that shivered every leaf on a branch—and
murmuring prayers of the black Friars Penitent who
accompany a criminal to the torture.

At last there were—thus ends the dream, this I tell—a monk
dying in the ashes of penitence, a girl who swung, hanged
from an oak branch, and I, bound spreadeagled by the
executioner on the spokes of the wheel.

Dom Augustin, the dead prior, will have full funeral honors in
the prayerful chapel; Marguerite, whom her lover murdered,
will be buried in her white innocent dress, between waxen
candles.

But I—, the executioner's blade broke like a glass at the first
blow; the penitent's torches drowned in floods of rain; the
crowd was swept away by rushing streams in spate—and I
followed other dreams to my waking.

---

† From GASPARD DE LA NUIT by Aloysius Bertrand
  translated from the French by Dudley Laufman

SCARBO [†]

My God, give to me at the hour of my death,
the prayers of a priest, a shroud of lined,
a bier of pine, and a dry place.

—The paternosters of M. le Marchal

Whether thou diest absolved or damned, muttered Scarbo that night in my ear, thou shalt have for a shroud a spider's web, and I shall bury the spider with thee.

—O, grant me at least for shroud, I answered him, my eyes red from much weeping, a leaf of aspen in which the breath of the lake will rock me.

—No, cackled the mocking dwarf; thou shalt be the pasture of the scarab-beetle that chases at night gnats blinded by the setting sun.

—Wouldst thou rather the-I said still weeping—wouldst thou rather I be bled by a spider with an elephant's snout?

—Well, he rejoined, console thyself. Thou shalt have for shroud the god-spotted bands of a snakeskin, in which I shall swaddle thee like a mummy.

And in the shadowy crypt of Saint-Benigne, where I shall stand thee upright against the wall, thou shalt forever hear the little unbaptized babes who weep in Limbo.

[†] From GASPARD DE LA NUIT by Aloysius Bertrand
translated from the French by Dudley Laufman

THE MASON †

The mason Abraham Kuffer sings, trowel in his hand, on the breezy scaffold where he steadies himself, so high that he could read the Gothic verse on the big bell of the thirty arched church in the town of thirty arches.

He sees the stone roof tiles spewing water in the cluttered abyss of galleries, windows, pendants, pinnacles, turrets, roofs and beams which the crescent still wing of the falcon marks with one gray point.

He sees the star shaped fortifications, the citadel that swells like an apple filling, the courts of the palace, the dried up fountains and the cloisters of the monasteries where the shadows move round the pillars

The imperial troops are quartered at the town's edge. There's a soldier drumming over there. Abraham Kuffer notices his three cornered hat, his epaulets of red wool, his cockade crossed with rosette and his pigtail tied with a bow.

What he sees next are some old soldiers who, in the part fringed with plumes of gigantic greenwood trees on wide green lawns, are shooting with their blunderbusses, at a wooden bird pinned to the top of a maypole.

And at night when the nave of the ringing cathedral sleeps, its arms crossed, he sees from the ladder, a village on the horizon, burned by soldiers, that blazed like a comet in the sky.

† From GASPARD DE LA NUIT by Aloysius Bertrand
translated from the French by Dudley Laufman

CHEVREMORTE †

*I was scratched by desert thorns
and every day I leave part of my body behind.*

—The Martyrs, Book X

It is not here that one breathes the moss of oaks or the bids of poplar, it is not here that the breezes and the waters murmur of love together.

No balm, in the morning after the rain, in the evening at the hour of dew, and nothing to charm the ear but the cry of the small bird in quest of a blade of grass.

The wilderness which no longer hears the voice of John the Baptist. Wilderness where no longer live the hermits or the doves.

So my soul is a solitude on the edge of the abyss, one hand in life, the other in death, I sob in desolation.

The poet is like the gillyflower which clings, weak and fragrant, to a rock, and asks less earth than sun.

But alas, I have no more sun, since closed are the charming eyes which warmed my genius.

---

† From GASPARD DE LA NUIT by Aloysius Bertrand
translated from the French by Dudley Laufman

HARLEM †

While the gold cock of Amsterdam sings,
The golden chicken of harlem lays eggs.

—Nostradamus (The Centuries)

Harlem, that admirable place of revelry which resembles the
Flemish School, Harlem as painted by Jean Breughel, Peter
Neef, David Taniers and Paul Rembrandt;

And the canal where the blue water trembles, and the church
where the gold window gleams, and the stone balcony where
the linen dries in the sun, and the hop green roofs;

And the storks which beat their wings around the clock of the
town, stretching their necks in the breezes and taking the
drops of rain in their beaks;

And the easy going burgomeister who rubs his double chin,
and the amorous florist who grows thin watching a tulip;

And the bohemian who swoons on his mandolin, and the old
rascal who plays on the Rommelpot, and the child who blows
a whistle;

And the drinkers who smoke in the one-eyed tavern, and the
servant in the butcher shop who hangs up a dead pheasant in
the window.

---

† From GASPARD DE LA NUIT by Aloysius Bertrand
translated from the French by Dudley Laufman

FIVE FINGERS OF THE HAND [†]

An honest family where no one has ever failed,
where no one has been hanged.

—The Family of John of Nivelle

The thumb is the fat Flemish publican, bantering and jolly,
who smokes by his gate under the signboard of the double
beers of March.

The index finger is his wife, a gaunt shrew, like an old fish,
who strikes the serving maid of whom she is jealous, and
caresses the bottle of which she is fond.

The middle finger is their son who has been whittled into
shape; he would be soldier if he were not bartender, and he
would be a horse if he were not a man.

The ring finger is their daughter, a supple Zerbine, who serves
the foamy laced draughts, but sells not her smiles to her
dandys.

And the ear finger is the baby of the family, a whining brat
who is always clinging to his mother's apron strings like a
small child hanging from the fang of an ogress.

The five fingers of the hand are the most marvelous five
petaled gillyflowers which have ever embroidered the flower
beds of the noble city of Harlem.

[†] From GASPARD DE LA NUIT by Aloysius Bertrand
translated from the French by Dudley Laufman

V.

Wee Herd's Whistle

THE FREIGHTER

Appears on the horizon
The heavy motors churn
across the waves on
vrooms and turns

Low hung it waits
at the harbor mouth
for the black and red tug boats
to come out

They guide it slowly
in by the wooded point
(Above the pine trees
float spars and joints)

She comes up the river
in the tug boat's wake
Makes my beer quiver
and the building shake

Up goes the bridge
Free drinks all around
Into the anchorage
to loom over the town

Unload the cargo—
gray salt in a pile

Crew out on leave now
inland for awhile

Walk out on the old town
take food and strong tea
Sleep in their cabins
safe from the sea

VINYL

They always start off with
Hello my name is Stan
how are you today
My boss says we have selected your house
to be a showcase for our product Vinyl Siding
To which you reply
I live in a stone dance hall
why would we want to put vinyl over that
So he goes on about all seasons windows
I tell him we have diamond paned
he tries the plastic roof
I tell him we have slate and he quits
Ten minutes later
woman from same place gives it a try
and you tell her you live in a
plastic inflated dome like a see through yurt
stays up with hot air from the dance hall
thatched canopy keep off snow
Then there's the septic guy
wants to pump out the tank
and you say *What tank*
And he asks *How do you dispose of you know what*
and you say *We live in a tree house*
the shit slides down a tube to a fan
which directs it to a fallow part of the garden

Have a good one he says

Last but not least is the newspaper
Manchester Onion Reader and you say
I haven't read that thing
since I started cutting my own hair
and I am not about to subscribe now
even if Billy Loeb and his old lady
are no longer with it if they ever were
But just out curiosity, how would you deliver it

Tube at driveway

Don't have a driveway
live in the woods on a pond fly in
Only get my mail once a week
at the post office where I hang out Saturday mornings
get paid to be town character couple hours
besides who wants to read week old newspapers

OLD SOUL

Lord knows how we become the way we are
Environment maybe
some from Mom Pop
grand parents both sides
distant relatives
Perhaps some ancient soul
eyeballs us from above
enters our being
becomes part of our make-up

I was a tornado in a past life
Big black thunderhead
full of passions lusts
                    I sent
                  my funnel
                   straight
                    down
                 to tear up
                  the turf
             enter the rolling ground
             Four or five times a week
             I couldn't get enough

Later in midlife I began to pull away from my base
leaving my snout
writhing and sniffing
below
my eyes bigger than my budelia

Eventually I began to rope out as they say in weather jargon
while old Buddy stayed
in the same place
doing his thing
grinding away as before

Finally I pulled out altogether
leaving my member to go it alone
best he could figure it out for himself

1/28/86

At the dump
a tin can
rockets
out of the fire

arcs
hissing into
a barrel of
water

Curious
I take it
from its deep
resting place

Through the
jagged hole
I see a nest
of fiber-glass

insulation
and seven
mice unseeing
eyes averted

I am
still holding
them

HANDS BEHIND

When I want to be a gentleman
I walk with my
hands behind my back
the left hand
grasping the other wrist
or just holding that hand
This is not meant for walking fast
A leisurely pace suits it
Allows time to stop
hands still behind back
to study a sapling
growing out of a banking
wondering if it would
make a walking stick
Or to talk with a companion
walking with me

Carrying a walking stick
does present a problem
I can walk with one hand
behind my back
or I can give the stick a rest
by holding it across my rump
with both hands on it

One leans forward
when walking hands clasped behind

Gives the impression
one has someplace to go
even slowly
It also makes one
pull in ones gut
makes one feel slim

THE WEDDING

Hey that's nothing
you shoulda seen what happen
at our wedding
We had it at the house
small private gathering
family friends you know
a JP pot luck canned music like that
and I'm standing there inna solarium
waiting to go downa isle
  we got a little alter
  by the bird bath see
'n Harris is down there
shootin the shit with the JP
an' the phone rings
Can you believe it
the phone rings
'n I'm thinking it's
some relative can't come
Pick it up *Hello*
'n this guy says *Harris there*
'n I say *he's busy*
'n the guy says
This is his boss
gotta speak to 'im now important
so I yell for Harris
Get up here yer boss onna phone
so Harris comes up

says *What I'm getting married*
'n hangs up
So I goes down the pathway
arm of Dad nice music playing
'n the JP says his stuff
'n gets to *For richer or poorer*
I'm standing there cracking up
'cuz Harris probably just got fired

THE CHILDREN

The children
came in
with an autumn
ash leaf

placed it
veins up
on the table

traced its
relief
in yellow
on a clean sheet
and sent it
to Aunt Bett
who was ailing

She fell from
her tree
that evening

A REGULAR GUY'S BONDING

You know what is really cool
is like when
he's driving down the street
and sees his buddy

Saw him this morning
at the store
but that's different

It's cool behind their wheels

They toot horns
wave laugh
shout Hey out the window
as they drive by

Like that's really cool

A MAINE CANOE GUIDE

≈ 1 ≈

She just loves them old fiddle tunes
Whistles them all the time
on the water and off
note for note and then some
with all the trills and grace notes
Has a long paddle made just for her
Stands up in the stern
plaid shirt leather vest jeans
red neckerchief wide brimmed hat
feather and a sprig of green in the band

Entertains her passengers
whistling jigs and reels in time to her
J-strokes and featherings
short for the jigs long for the hornpipes
OVER THE WAVES for the slow wakes
LIFE ON THE OCEAN WAVE or SAILOR'S HORNPIPE
after the speedboats pass
RIPPLING WATER JIG in the rapids
and OVER THE WATERFALL in plenty of time
for the ride easy as ROLLING OFF A LOG

≈ 2 ≈

Last year
she got her deer
from her canoe

standing up
Nearly tipped over
trundling the doe
into the bark
cussing and praying
at the same time

This year she took her stand
perched twenty feet up a pine
above a well known run
A float plane flew by low overhead
back and forth shying the deer
She knew who it was,
that big spender from the east
Shook her fist at the sky
saying *Damn you drop dead*
Silence after that but no deer
An hour or so later
she heard sirens in the distance
thought nothing of it
Got home found out that
he had crashed his plane
on an island in the lake
he was ok but wrecked the plane
Serves him right the old poop

Next day from her blind in the air
she nailed a neat buck

They had the liver for supper
over an open fire

Pays sometimes to shake your fist up

≫ 3 ≈

She and her husband
live in a wall tent
edge of the Big Walters Stream
Has a wood floor
Franklin stove four posted bed
picture window looks out on the water
sit there candle light glass of wine
Easily a mile downhill from the road
tote everything in on their backs

Her dad worries says
How you going to manage all this
when you get older can't
carry a deer miles out of the bush
You going to move into your canoe barn
up the road winterize it

She says *You know*
I haven't really thought about it
Guess we'll go over that waterfall
when we come to it

DIORAMAS

are fascinating
like the ones at Concord Massachusetts
depicting the battle at the bridge
Or the three at Widner Library
Harvard University with details of Harvard Square
from the 1600s to the 1930s

I made one to scale
of a dairy farm
on our ping-pong table
The neighborhood boys didn't like it because
when they wanted to play gnip-gnop
they had to take it down and put it back
just the way I had it before
They quit altogether when I got
real cowshit to enhance the scene

I made another of Fenway Park
on my bedroom floor
complete with the green monster

But I was blown away
when visiting Germany in 2005
by the four in the Old Town Hall
in Hannover Germany
The first one is set in 1605
a medieval city surrounded by a

star moat farms and forest on the edge
Next is 1939 a burgeoning city
complete with railroad church steeples
red roofs predominate in miniature detail
merging into the painted horizon
Next one dated 1945
the city is dull brown and gray ash
Just gable ends and cellar holes brick rubble
The railroad station roof is full of holes
Only the church and Town Hall remain

We stood there heads bowed
Even though we didn't do it
we somehow felt responsible

A man next to us said
Terrible isn't it
He was short and balding
smiling hesitantly
Said *One good thing that came out of the war*
was that we kinder could explore the ruins
He said *Every night the sirens would sound*
we would take a blanket and go to underground

He told us his brother came home
with a bullet hole in one cheek and out the other
They patched it up in hopes to

heal and stay home
but he was sent back to the front
Never saw him again
Not a word

He said *Mother looked like Marlene Deitritch*
Father was killed
at the Battle of the Bulge
In two years Mother
had aged to being
stooped and gray

He held his clenched
hands beside his head
squeezed his eyes shut
saying *I hate war*
I chust hate war

THIS WOMAN

it's hard to believe she did what she did
Inherited the family place on the shore
down there Westerly Rhode Island
big place like an estate
Spent her summers there as a kid
hated to leave in the fall
go back to Indianapolis or
wherever it was out there someplace
cry carry on

But she stays out there
school house job husband you know

Then she chucks everything
job house marriage
comes east
winterizes the shore place
retaining wall against the line storms
shutters against hurricanes
spent a fortune
Says she is going to move in
write paint soak up the shore
talk to the locals knowingly about lobstering
be part of the community

So what does she do but get a job
a good job mind you

don't blame her there
up in Worcester
Good bucks but doesn't like the commute
what seventy-five miles
so she buys a big town house
moves in
tells everyone at parties
all there is to know about Worcester

Hits the shore only on occasional weekends
She keeps it like a delayed orgasm
and last summer she goes to France
gets to the shore once
cries when she leaves

WINNING

Up north there's a place
they play a kind of baseball
that anyone and everyone can play
scattered around the field
various positions catcher pitcher

Batter stays up til he or she
hits the ball fair or foul
and runs like hell around the bases
and out onto the field
making room for another batter

Fielders go through the motions
triple plays stretchy windups
but no umps although one time
they pulled the local mountie
in to take his raps

No scratching the crotch
or lengthy confabs on the mound
no bullpens or fences
Everybody wins

IF A LITTLE MAN

If a little man
danced in a circle of goats
who would hug him

THIS IS THE WAY

This is the way the lady rides
shuttle the kids
off to the school
down to the library
up to the rink
down to the pool

And this is the way her husband rides
out in the moonlight
isn't he cool
isn't he cool

And this is the way the gentleman rides
cadilac cadilac cadilac

And this is the way the farmer rides
off to the bank to pick up a check
for another good cow
to make more manure
to spread on the land
to make more hay
to feed to the cows
to make more milk
to sell to the co-op
for another good cow
and pay the grain bill

And this is the way the cowboy rides
and this little private went AWOL
and this corporal went on a spree
and this sergeant said get in order
and this John Doe said not me
and this man cried all the way home in his sleep
for shooting a kid on the street

And this is the way the baby rides
innocently innocently innocently

BALLOONS AT A WEDDING

They were
cast off
fifty or more
surging aloft

into the rain.
Twenty-five or so
chose to remain
below

behind bushes
standing on strings
watching us
dance sing

cut the cake
One by one
they make
it off the lawn

gently assisted
by toe or palm
into the mist—
quickly gone.

WEE HERD'S WHISTLE

Tanu has no
herd to call

but we
know where

he is
now

Someday I'll
find it in

an eave box
with no herd

to whistle
either

HISTORY OF A FLOOR

The floor stones are rough and uneven
sloping to the central large stone
which is three feet at its widest
four feet going the other way
and concave like a valley floor
for the other stones to drain into
We found this stone on the boundry wall
had chisel marks from the Shaker quarry
Flat and only three inches thick
We end over ended it into place
in its bed of sand
fanning the other stones out from it
mortaring them with cement rivers
It looked like a map of Islandia

I wanted the whole house built of stone
but the floor was all I managed
being impatient and pushed for time
with November drawing to a close
and ready cash running out as well
A wooden house was what we made
heavy beams and wide board walls
fireplace built of cobblestones

My daughter Windy when she was seven
batted a ball around the floor
with a sawed off hockey stick
whacking it off the window seats

eventually sinking one into
the fireplace stick raised high
nearly clouting the chandelier
while shouting *Score number four
Bobby Orr and his sister Espisito*

The neighbors' kids would play hopscotch
on one foot from stone to stone
and they still do when they come in
even though they are fifty or more

I keep my house plants on the stones
water them with spray and stream
like in a greenhouse or outdoors
water pooling on the rocks
under moist geraniums

We have danced upon this floor
the big slab like a battering stone
in an Irish set from County Clare
A little corn meal to smooth the dance
the swings the left hand allemands

About this time a bank was robbed nearby
Two state troopers
lord knows why
came here to question me

upon my whereabouts
during that robbery
wanting to know what I did with the loot
hinting it was under the stones
We sent them packing
They never returned

Another man with good intentions
measured the floor for rug or plywood
to make it warmer for his grandchild
Thanks I said to him But no thanks

My son Nathaniel five years old
came up to visit from his mother's
in wintertime
She'd gone to Florida for a week
left him with me
He sat alone on the cold floor
on the big stone by the fire
He sniffed back tears and then began
uncontrollable wracking sobbing
I knelt to hold him he pushed back
turned his face away from me

I could not get him come to supper
He sat there a little Indian
wrapped in a blanket sucking his thumb

PRIDE IS A BITTER PILL

Pride is a hard and bitter pill to swallow
having to take back a firm decision
like swearing to be a lifetime vegetarian
or follow the simple life like Thoreau

I said I'd do without machines forever
Dig my fields by spade and cut my fuel
by hand and tote my crops by wheelbarrow
unbothered by machines Never say never

Children grow and shoes and teeth are costly
Time is shorter and my muscles grow weary
Meat seems good chain saws cut more quickly
Thoreau was single the simple life seems hollow
I make excuses as I succumb to progress
but pride is still a bitter pill to swallow

And yet though pride may be a bitter pill
does not mean that I have given up
Today tomorrow I'll still try to cut
my stove wood with a buck saw and to till
my fields in one manner or another
and hope that woodsmoke clings to my clothing
rich and pungent and that the wind will sing
on my face again over and over

I would hope to keep in my own employ
singing jigs for coins poems for joy

Perhaps I will become a wandering minstrel
pastoral still but restless all quite strange
to me who has roots down that are rural

The only permanence we know is change

SHAKER GHOSTS

Once these broad green rolling fields were hayed
By rugged Shaker men tandemmed across
The meadow
                    scythes swishing through the grass
They would stop under the welcome shade
Of spreading elm to drink from jars of switchel

Then the day would sing with metalled song
Of whetstones on dew wet scythes until
The distant hills sent the echo along

Today the farmer sits astride his steed
Of steel and mows the swath in golden rows
Followed by the whirling rake that feeds
The gulping hay baling machine that follows
Beer drinking men bring in the harvest
While leaning on their scythes are Shaker ghosts.

SKATING THE SHAKER PONDS

There was an inn in the trees where the
woodcutters stopped to drink, and we sat inside by the
stove,
drank hot red wine with spices.

—Hemingway, A Farewell To Arms

There are six ponds in the Shaker woods,
All within walking distance of each other
   and from us as well,
Not to mention a seventh, mile and a bit below.
All connected by ditches.

One day in December some time ago
   before the snow came,
We had a spell of cold weather.
Mercury dropped to ten scratches
Beneath the hole for three nights running.
Morning of the fourth day
Snow was predicted by nightfall,
Fact was, the sky was yellow gray by eleven.
Gonna skate, gotta do it now.

Through the woods up to the North Pond.
Long and narrow, Glimmerglass smooth.
We skated the length in two minutes,
Off with skates and through some bony marsh
Onto Runaway, the largest of the seven
   with an island to go around twice, then
Race down the middle to the dam.

*

Skates off and over a trail to the earth dam
    east end of Fountain, putting in,
Skirting the shore to the spillway end.
Boots on and along the pine needled
    woods road to the
Cluster of three ponds below the Village.
Snow starting.

Around the top one quick.

Tip toe on skate points to the middle pond
    shaped like a four-leaf clover.

Over the dam dropping right onto the lower pond,
Skating into a snow swirl that skimmed the ice,
    starting to stick to the shore.

We called it quits.

Inch of snow on the ground by the time we got home.
Buttered up hot rum and maple syrup
Sprinkled with cinnamon,
    sat by the stove saying,
We should do that again, take in Carding Mill too.

But we never have.
That was twenty years ago.

THE EVENING HORSES

The evening horses came
wind blew the leaves inside out

All night
          dogs barked
slivers of
          moonlight & teeth

WALKING STICKS

A cannister full by the front door
    with some umbrellas
(one ivory handled for the Colonel)
the others all waiting to go out
Cherry Apple Ash
smoothed by use and time

They jostle for position
    hoping for the warm hand
        around their neck

They know where to go

THE ONE EYED SINGER

for Alan
January 7, 2001

A winter afternoon with snow piled against the stone church, and holly, poinsettias and candles set in the deep window casements. Fur coats and tweeds were in ample evidence, a comfortable company for your funeral.

The organ, with all stops pulled, made the alleluias ring in the arches, striking those chords that make tears flow.

The white robed choir came down the granite-paved aisle, singing Praise To God:

When in our music God is glorified...

Your cats and other timid folks you have known were not to be seen, probably curled in a fur collar or disguised in a Harris.

Then...there was one...in the choir. The skirt of his gown barely covering his work shoes, holding the hymnal an inch from his eyes, moving his face from side to side, smiling tentatively, singing for you.

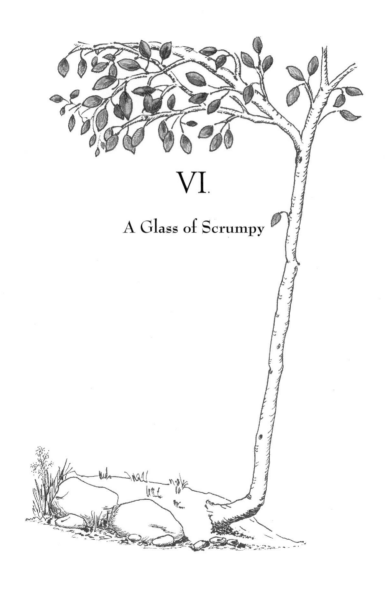

VI.

A Glass of Scrumpy

1-2-3 REDLIGHT

You wouldn't believe it to see it now
but we had wheat growing here
corn for bread field beans
every inch was cultivated
no weeds even around the rocks
what we didn't get the goats did

View from the kitchen window
looked out over the woods
to the forested hillside three miles away

Now I turn my back on the garden
Hasps of grass and wild roses
creep towards the house
When I turn around they stop
look again they have advanced a foot
respecting only the onions and potatoes
Soon one or two of them
will reach the house before I count 3
Somehow this is comforting
The garden is now an island in a sea of timothy
narrow trodden paths wending
to the garlic or the token row of peas

At morning coffee there is no view
Apple trees have taken over
reaching out towards the house
They are our friends our children
all crowding in to take us in their arms

THE CALENDAR ACCORDING TO DUDLEY

Okay you know that
June 21 is Midsummer
summer solstice
at least in Sweden it is
It means that the days
start getting shorter then
Okay so then it stands to reason
that December 21 is midwinter
winter solstice and the
days start getting longer
So okay if December 21 is midwinter
when is the FIRST day of winter
Well count back six weeks
and you have Halloween
as first day of winter
Then six weeks the other way
from December 21 gives you
February 2 *Candlemas Day*
Ground Hogs Day
half yer hay half yer wood
burn the solstice greens
and the first day of spring
St. Patrick's Day or thereabouts
is spring equinox
six weeks down the road
puts you at May Day
and the first day of summer

that's what they call it in England
Another six weeks or so
finds us at midsummer
How can it be FIRST day of summer
if the days start getting shorter
I've seen it snow June 21
worn a T-shirt and shorts December 21
Makes sense doesn't it
Beginning of August
is first day of autumn
mid-September fall equinox
and then Halloween
first day of winter
that's when all the old souls appear
wanting solace before the cold

KNOWING WHEN

Knowing when
to harvest a pear

is like knowing when
to pull in the oars

gliding to a pier

SWEARING

GOSHAMICKLE, DILLYPICKLE,
GEEWILLIWOBBLES, DOG MY CATS
& ROWREBAZZLE

—Pogo

Haywagon tipped over
spilling the load into the brook
Had to spread it all out to dry
Hot muggy day sweaty work
Twisted the hitch when the wagon tipped

Cows were ornery wouldn't come in
Some went cavorting back to pasture
had to go fetch them again

Milking time machines sucking away
radio going announces tornado in Worcester
One cow has to be stripped by hand
kicks the full pail over wraps
her wet tail around Bucky's head
He says *D O dash cuss O blank*
Never swears Never heard him swear
Most patient man One time he had to
shoot a cat got stepped on by a cow
Buried her in the barnyard tamping
down the earth I heard a meow thought
it was the cat…it was Bucky saying goodbye

Then the storm came We watched
through the barn windows as a red funnel
came up through the pasture
Took down the chicken house
spread it across the yard
Sucked up all the hay by the brook
dropped kicked them pine trees
across the meadow

COW BELLS

In the morning
you could tell
when he let the cows out
after milking
one or two at a time
by their bells clanking singly
as they headed off
to their day's work of making milk

Occasionally during the day
the sound would ring
up the valley to here
from a pasture knoll
or shaded hollow
by the brook

But at evening when he
called the cows for milking
Boss boss boss c'boss c'boss
the whole herd would
toll across the meadow
one hundred and twenty
Brown Swiss bells in a
cacophony of copper and brass

WINTER IN WISCONSIN

Sunday afternoon skverdans
in a Grange hall near Mineral Point
surrounded by rolling hills
that go on and on

Last dance of the day and
I'm finding folks to fill out the sets

Fiddle under arm
I approach the coat rack where
two girls are putting on their jackets

C'mon it's the last one
need you to round it out

Oh we're really sorry they said
but we have to go home to milk
and we are already late
fifty black and whites await us

They arranged their long yellow hair
outside their collars
a faint sweet smell of cow
reaching me

TO KEEP A COW

If you put your mind to it
you could keep a cow or two

Have a parcel of land
    a pond
Pour a slab build a lean-to
off the side of the house
big enough for two Jersey tie-ups
storage space for fodder
five ton bedding too old hay

Clear some brush for a paddock
build a wooden fence
Cut green feed with a scythe
toss over the fence in summer
Manure to neighbor exchange for hay

Make lightly salted sour cream butter
cottage cheese to sell at the door

One Jersey might make 10 quarts a day
that's 2 & 1/2 gallons which will yield about
a quart of cream = 1/2# butter   x 2   (the other cow)
that's a pound of butter a day
Skim milk to large curd cottage cheese
drink buttermilk
whey on compost

Quart of milk weighs 2 #   x 10 quarts = 20#
x 2 (other cow) = 40#
Feed 1# grain per 10# milk = 4# grain per day
25 days to go through a bag @ $14
Say a bag a month approximately 50¢ a day
Get 5 bucks for the butter and cheese
that's $5 a day—the grain = $4.50

Don't figure the labor it's a lifestyle
supposed to be enriching
Like they say put your mind to it

SILO

God awful hot
that day in June
putting up grass silage

Coming in with a load
we could hear a cracking sound
coming from the barn

Got there found the silo
split wide open
steaming silage and splintered wood
spread out on the barnyard

Evans took a wad of bills from his pocket
doled out some to each of us
Said *Hell wivvit*
take the rest of the day boys
Sox double header 'safternoon
We'll clean this up tomorrow

SILAGE GONE

at the end of February
poorish hay left to carry over

Milk production down

Had to buy extra to cover
the door to door milk route

Picked up forty quarts from a neighbor
every other day
They fed their black and whites
on slop from the brewery in Somersworth
Put it on the hay the grain the silage
Dried brewery slop stuck to the mangers
the barrels it came in, their truck
A sweet beery smell mixed in with
the hay manure and silage

Their road was not plowed
Had to walk down pulling a sled

In the tie-up the backs of the Holsteins
touched the low rafters of the old barn
The stoop-shouldered neighbor said
Anyone who works here
must have their back bent

We pulled the forty quart jug of milk
balanced on the sled
half a mile uphill
through a foot of snow
in the dark

Back home dumped the milk
into the tank
mixing it with the Jersey milk
Had some at supper
Tasted beery
Father wouldn't touch his
Went down to the barn
squirted some fresh milk
from a few cows
brought it up for his supper
Drank it warm

PAUL

Should see that kid inna next cabin
he's all freckles
skinny glasses buck teeth
bet he has freckles on 'is you know what

I went down to the beach
there he was playing in the sand
with a toy Ford tractor

Seersucker overalls railroad cap
glasses holding up the visor
had to look under them to see me

Held out his fist to shake
couldn't open it said *I'm Paul*
Troop 16 Lexington

Yeah, I'm Willy Troop 1
Arlington Mass Ave there

Across the lake was a juniper studded pasture
dotted with black and white cows
Holsteins I say
Best cows says Paul *most milk*

Naw Jerseys says I *best milk*

How'd you know
Arlington   no cows there

Oh yeah we have three jerseys
right up under your nose there on the line
sell yellow milk at the door
How's it you know Holsteins

We milk hundred-fifty
our farm right on the street in town
buy our hay from Quebec
peddle product in glass   door to door
Dad does it all   even crippled like me
Brother does the milking
he's a hippie   has long hair
won't have to go to war
neither will I

HOW TO MAKE A SEMEN COLLECTOR

Take a tractor 2" radiator hose about 2' long
and a bicycle tire inner tube
Cut out a 3' section to slide down inside the hose
leaving 6" out at each end
At one end fold the tube back over the hose
securing it with a rubber band
Do the same at the other end
but before you do
pour some hot water (100 degrees)
between tube and hose
and seal it in as above
Then take your test tube and rubber flange
slide it over one end and secure
Astroglide jelly up the other end
Now you're ready for the bull
When he goes to mount the cow
slip the rig over his budelia
and Bob's your uncle

HAYMOW IN FEBRUARY

Feed is half gone

Hip roof yawns
                    above me

protruding shingle nails
                              starwhite
with frost

Downstairs
                a cow jangles
her stanchion

Hay is cold
                peeling off
                              in thin layer

FARM

I wore sleeveless undershirts
and railroad caps
because the men did

Cows came home single file—
(sweet fern pine needles iced tea)

Before supper Bucky said
For these and all thy cardinal flowers to us
we give thee thanks
in Jesus name amen

Silky greenfeed slid down the shoot
All the Jerseys looked up
their noses moist as snails

Afterwards stood around the kitchen
in our undershirts
breaking chocolate icebox cookies
into glasses of milk

DAIRY

A pair of ankle length rubber boots
on an overturned milk can

Water evaporating on the bronze cement

On the shelf
a jar of disinfectant
a piece of pipe
a dirty cream bottle from
some dairy down in Rhode Island

Speared from a nail—a note
  Please leave 1 extra qt for next 3 wks we will
  have fresh air child w/ us   thanks   R Beede

Through the open door
    a green and yellow truck
    ice melting from empty crates

A GLASS OF SCRUMPY AT THE GEORGE

Them trees is one of our best kept secrets
even we don't always know
where they is until the cows
show us the way in the fall
then later by the burlap bags
bulging with scrumpy apples
leaning against the trees

Get good crops we do

In January hang strips of
gin soaked toast from the twigs
pour a little around the roots

I have to suck in my breath
at such a waste but it works

Get loads of apples

Barrels full, bins full 'til they overflow
and the cyder runs out of every gutter hole
says the old song

And we fires off a shotgun blast into the night
scare off evil spirits

Oh don't pay no nevermind
to them brown flecks floating around
they just be from inside the cask

Well here's to ye—cheers

HEADSTONE

Maybe seventy five
hundred years ago
a line storm
blew down a big tree
in the woods
up on the hill above
St. Catherine Ayers Cliff
In falling it left a
big hole prying up
its own headstone
a thick granite slab
standing straight up
at the end of the hole
Bury me there
said Real Boushell
that's where I want to lie
Mon dieu that old wind
sure screwed some
grave diggers out of a job eh

SOYBEAN

I helped a farmer in Ohio
harvest soybeans brown and brittle
The field was two miles long at least
and one mile at the widest
Took an hour to get around

After two passes we stopped
at a Dunkin Donuts for a cup of coffee
Left the combine running at the field's edge
He said *I can tell you what each*
farmer here in Van Wert County
has planted for corn or soybeans
what variety of seed stock
just by looking at the crop

Later he had me disc in stubble
with a John Deere tractor that
was equipped with air conditioning
stocked with M & Ms and CDs
First I had to measure off
the area I was to harrow
Put a marker at each corner
an orange flag stuck on a wire
which when pushed into the soil
kept going without resistance
The farmer said the topsoil had
a depth of twenty feet or more

He visited us in New Hampshire
Took him to the beach at Rye
had a beer in Kittery
showed him through the White Mountains
He marveled at it all but had
trouble with the woods and forests
They all look the same he said
How do you find your way home

MID-SPRING IN CONNECTICUT

About nine to ten miles
north of New Haven
maybe a couple miles
east of Route 91
you get into some
high open country
roller coaster land
steep curvy roads
like Wisconsin or
Georgeville Quebec
dairy farms with silos
black and whites
waiting for evening milking

A cold front
is moving in
low gray clouds
with the setting sun
streaming in underneath
hue-ing the leafless trees
the meadows
the barn windows
a brilliant copper

A whiff of woodsmoke
mingles with manure
and corn silage

Scarlatti on the CD
I turn it up full

We are going out to dinner.

LONGJOHNS

We only do things in season.
Much more fun that doing things in reason.

—Newt Tolman
from OUR LOONS ARE ALWAYS LAUGHING

I put mine on the morning of Thanksgiving
or if I'm up
the night before

Sometimes it's so warm I wish I hadn't
but a ritual is a ritual

They stay on come hell or high water
throughout the winter only coming off
for showers or sex and not always for that

This goes on until the first of April
or if I'm up
the night before

Sometimes it is so cold I wish
I had kept them on but a ritual is

The old man at the dairy farm where I
used to work wore his all year around
A one piece union suit then it was called
with a trap door flap over his butt

that he unbuttoned when he took a dump
Same in summer except the top was short sleeved
I guess he just got used to wearing them
and was not burdened by a ritual
except to change from long sleeve into short

The old men at New Hampshire Hospital
wore longjohns the year around as well
Got a little rank by shower time
My friend Arthur Hanson bragged about it
New longies or clean ones every week
Wintertime they keep old frosty out
and summer time ward off the heat

Maybe I'll get me one of them one piece suits
Must remember to unbutton the flap

BOBBIN AT THE BEEBE RIVER

You can see the place
through the trees in winter
otherwise you wouldn't
know it was there
An abandoned mill village
row houses
most of them empty boarded up
but in summer
some with flowers and lawn
beat up cars in yard
kids running in and out of sagging doors
Road full of holes
does a 45
and goes along side the railroad track
by a burnt out post office
towards the bobbin factory
broken widows no roof
They made bobbins for cotton mills
'til the industry moved south
Does another 45 around a pond
sawmill with gaping ragged hole
like a log got shot through
More vacant faced kids
like in DELIVERANCE
Time to get out of there
but have to drive by the local industry
a coffin factory

with a big bonfire of tires in the yard
Up the hill through an open field
pity the poor kids in winter
getting off the bus
trudging head down
into that blast from Canada

TEASING THE WAVES

is when you
stand on a rock at high tide
wearing your good shoes
not gortex
jumping back before the wave

Teasing the cold is when you
see how far into October you can get
before you have to
shut the windows in the house
how far into fall before you
have to make a fire in the stove
have to keep a fire going overnight

Teasing the North is when you
drive as far as you can
north of Lac St Jean
past Sainted Lakes
before you run out of road

Teasing the snow is when you
head east into the woods
the wind out of the northeast
sky yellowish gray spitting snow
see how far you can go
before you decide it might be a
good idea to turn around
head for home

VII.

On the Edge of the Burren

BEES

have taken up residence
buzzing behind the wall of our bathroom

Tapping the wall with the butt of my razor
made them buzz louder
and suddenly the room was full of them
whirling around my head

I ducked out
grabbed some Raid
and hit them hard
dropping them left and right
before I realized they had not stung me
              even attacked me
It was as if they were playing with me
              just curious
Now I noticed they were small yellow bees
wild honey bees writhing in the sink
I am so sorry I said to them
What kind of host am I
How may I atone
Sting me a few times

They did not seem to want to
I'll gather up your dead
give them a decent burial among the phlox
Put out a dish of honey so those we zapped
          may die a sweet death

161

A beekeeper friend said
These are not bees
but rather some kind of
wasp hornet yellow jacket
They will die over winter
if you can wait that long
If they aren't aggressive
consider yourself lucky

Does this information really change anything
Because they are not bees
does this give me license to zap them again

WATER

Folks said if you want water
get in touch with Adam Pingree
but you'll have to drive him
he don't have a car

So I go up there old farm house
wood stove going middle of summer
dirty dishes in sink
canyons through the piles of newspapers

Tell him I need water
get yer dowsing sticks
He says *Don't need em*
don't travel anymore
let's make a map
'cuz I don't know your place
Sharpens his pencil
draws the house the septic
the rise of land back of barn
makes squiggly lines
wavering across the paper
where the hill slopes down
coming together near the house
says *There's water there*
No need for me to come out
ten bucks will do fine

The backhoe man has a set
of those metal dowsing rods
He finds water exactly where
Adam says it is

Starts to dig
hole fills in with water
faster'n he can scoop it out

Reminds him of the time
folks wanted a well in their yard
close to the house
tired of hauling water from town

Backhoe man says
Adam Pingree's yer man

Never been over that part of the county
says Adam *but I kin tell you*
there is a well in yer cellar
been there since the house was built

Sure enough there was
and a good one at that
cover 'n all
good clear water

FIXING AN OLD HOUSE

They were working on their place
right after they moved in
His wife says *This is an old house*
must have some big rough beams
So he rips down the plaster over the kitchen
Found some thick poles bark still on em
going every which way
holding up the floor above
Contractor working with him
found an old shoe amongst the poles
squared off at the toe had copper nails
Said *Folks in them days*
put a shoe in the rafters for good luck
Here put it on yer mantle

No put it back we'll keep the luck

Covered it up
notched in some floaters
six bys hung baskets from them

Later working outside
an old lady stops says
I used to live here back fifty years ago
husband and I just married

Would you care to come in he asked
No she said Not No thank you

but just plain and blunt No
as she went her way

Several years later five maybe
He's out there doing the lawn
she comes by bent over
asks can she come in
Said *Husband and I lived here in this room*
another couple had the kitchen
and a whole family lived over the woodshed
Crowded but we all got along

He heard she died a week later
Never found out why she wouldn't come in
that first time

DOUBLE HEADER

The dog chased a ball
through the outfield of the garden all afternoon
returning it slavered
to wait patiently for someone to throw it back
In the swamp beyond
a great blue heron
hidden by the ghosts of dead trees
stalked a trout all afternoon
finally getting it
to the applause of all watching
Steve said *I spend a small fortune feeding that bird*
The great blue launched itself
skimming the marsh grass
to another fishing spot
hidden among stumps
Its flight attracted the dog
Leaving the ball he hell bent it for the bird
us yelling *Come back*
Not to worry soon we saw the slow
up and down of the gray wings
against the dark green of the forest

SWARM

A golden bee map of New England
and a bit of Quebec plastered
the side of the garden house
They's goin' to go
and go they did
a whirlwind of bronze Zs and Xs
They's gonna settle on the lilac
and settle they did
a pulsating ball
Has someone died here
If someone dies and
you don't tell the bees
they'll leave and they have
Old wives tale

Lois came down in the morning
dressed for church high heels
trundling a wheelbarrow
with a bushel basket in it
Putting it under the lilac
she shook the branch
and the bees thlumped into the basket
Lois said *I'll come get them after Meeting*
put 'em in a new hive

PERFECT STORM

Working up
a good sweat
I skirt the side
of a steep hill
through slash
and stumps
the green ocean
of forest
sloping off
to the sides

Down into a
deep trough
looking up
to see a
hughmongous
wave looming
above me
blocking the sun.

I climb up and up
salt in my mouth
leveling off

PIG

Farmer has a sow in heat, puts her in wheelbarrow, trundles her to the boar. She comes around in a month, same drill. Next month she's around again, farmer gets his coat, comes out and the sow is already in the barrow.

Never forget that time
she had to get that boar pig Truffles
to service her Esmarelda sow

Drive down from Antrim
in that beat up old VW bus
flowers painted on the side

She pulled everything out of the back
piled bales of hay behind the seat
load Truffles in back
He's big as a couch and with tusks

She's driving along cold winter day
the bales shift a bit
and there's Truffles
sitting on the seat beside her
snout at the window
'n you know them ole VWs
windows frost right over
She's got a little peep hole
and Truffles has his

Driving along slowly
'n the old blue light is going behind her

She pulls over
Statie comes up says
I've stopped you for driving obstructed view
Looks in sees Truffles
doubles over with laughter
bends right over the hood

When he recovers she says
what am I to do
you see the hay bales
he just shoved them aside

Trooper gasps *Just go home lady*
just go home

So they make it somehow
and she opens the passenger door
Truffles gets right out
trots over to Esmerelda
does the job

OLD FELLER

He Remembers

See those dead branches there
'mongst the green of that old maple
Wicked wind came through here
July sometime back
snow hail whirling around
didn't see any funnel
but something dipped down
took a bite out of the center of that tree
shingles and drain pipe off the house
spread them across the road
So I says to the tree I says
Old tree if you survived that
I'll not be taking you down for firewood
and there she stands to this day
kind of funny looking but hey
so am I no hair creaky limbs

At The Races

You can hear them going at it
'bout a mile or so from here
especially if there is a
low cloud cover
and the wind is east

Keep thinking I should
get over to one sometime
but the other day
two fellers in pickups
burned rubber on the straight here
front of the house
Brought the race to me
Wasn't that nice of 'em

And Traffic

When I first came here to live
this road was gravel
Hardly any traffic
Truck or two
or horse drawn wagon
once or twice a day
Then they gave it a farmer's mix
putting blacktop over that
Now the cars go whipping by
every minute
or so it seems
Look at this now
here they come
one going one way one the other
Two cars at once
Whew what is this old world coming to

IN A HURRY

Surging up the driveway
  dew flying off the hood
    get to the post office
      before the mail goes
thinking of all to be done

The tiger lilies
in their orange vests
lean out
             flag me down

INLAND

On the grass stripped lane going up to Sam's
probably say fifty miles inland
the prow of a lobster boat plowed out
between the crotch of a scrub white birch
What is Sam up to now I thought
breast stroking my way through the bracken
to see how long the apparition was
Found it sawed off squarely
right behind the cabin
Asked him about it next day at the store
Said *You going lobstering or what*
and he said *Naw I'm just a part owner*

Month or so later by there again
and the hull is out on its side in the road
I asked *You forget to tie it up last storm*

Yeah but actually my snow plow
tipped it out into the lane
I should drag it up to the house
turn it over 'n keep hens in it

Talk about towing it in the snow
we used to take a flat bottomed row boat
and tow it behind my uncle's pickup
We'd all pile in with a beer or two
keep the chain loose and away we'd go

riding up the side of the bankings
from one side of the road to the other
Helluva time   I wouldn't mind
doing it again find an old boat
I've no points against my license

GIVEN

that you own your house and land
   mortgage free
and, given you have a thirty foot well
   that never goes dry and
given that your house is insulated
   warm and tight
and given you have garden space for
   potatoes onions beans
   (should all hell break loose) and
given that you know how to glean
   from garden dump and roadside
   as well as from the works of Thoreau
   Nearing etc what applies to you
   taking the rest with a grain of salt
and given you have access to a wood
   lot for three cords a year and
   to cash from work of some sort
   be it logging carpentering fishing
   fiddling whatever to pay for
   insurance taxes car to get you
   to said jobs in the first place and
given that you like northern winters
and most important that your kids are
   grown and gone or stayed
     and rooted
and even more important, that you
   have a rooted partner
then by god given all these givens
you should be able to cut it
   in the country

HIPPIES

Jesum they only have one room to live in
well a loft overhead
but really just one room
electricity but no running water
hand pump
wood burning cook stove
heats as well
crimus everything in the one room
even had their goats in there at one time
and my friend Tom
he sleeps in the loft under the eaves
sister has a room off to the side
so does his mom and pop
baby sleeps with them
jesoe the mom has all those diapers to do by hand
no toilet it's outside middle of winter
No car Mom stays home
dad dig ditches plays fiddle
walks to gigs bums a ride hitches
Poor says Tom
Says he doesn't want that life
wonders how long the mom'll stay
Grow a large garden jeeze
it's still green with stuff
kale leeks cabbage they don't do meat
lotsa soups like
and plenty of homemade bread

with butter from their goat's milk
golly it was good but
glad we don't live like that
no tele no McDonalds
Tom's never been to a MacDonalds
says when he has a car he'll go
have a thick shake like we all talk about,
his folks say that stuff's not good for you
He respects them but wants to find out
Sort of reminds me of what you talk about in church
'bout folks living simple off the land
maybe sort of like LITTLE HOUSE ON THE PRAIRIE
It was nice at supper with candles
they do have electricity I told you that
soup in wooden bowls
no noise from phones or tele
but christmas it seems
they just don't have a pot to piss in

COYDOGS

make a horizontal
circular song
at night

from the forest
or meadow
trotting silently

from place to place
sitting on haunches to sing
little ones yipping

around the edges
stopping suddenly
something entering their midst

APPLES

are good blended up
with bananas dates peanut butter
a little maple syrup

Or nibbled on
driving home late
help keep awake

We have a tree a semi-dwarf
yields two-three bushels
good yellow winter keepers

Cull them over weekly
tossing the brown ones
right up to the last apple

Like to say Have apples
all winter right through March
even though I don't eat them

THAT TRAIL

That trail
goes up through the town forest

I'm up there walking along
almost tumble into a cellar hole
covered with vines
didn't see it
would a been a ten foot fall

Got around that
came to what appeared to be
a coconut shell cut in half
level with the ground

turns out to be a ground hornets' nest
filled with pissed off yellows
just missed stepping on it
goddamit to hell anyway

Not much further on
came to a big black snake across the path
musta been two inches around
three foot long
It slithered off under a juniper
I heard a dry quivering
got the hell out of there

Later asked a Fish & Game guy
he said *Yes there are black rattlers in New Hampshire*
Like that time in the House
there was an article to offer bounty on rattlers
Turned down
 no rattlers in the state says the House
Man sponsoring the bill
came in the next day with a burlap sack
dumped four rattlers on the senate floor
and the bill passed

WHEELBARROWS

make good poems.
I have chalked
up two and have a
third in the works

When the kids asked
Bill where I went
with it always empty
he said probably poems

But it was most likely
four foot wood though
which I burned—my poems
don't come in feet now

Tim asked today
What are you getting
I said *The sides are down*
so poems won't stay in

nor sawdust must be
wood in straighter
lengths which I'll burn and come
back for the poems later

IN THE HAMMOCK

Westerly end hitched to an elm
sunrise end to a wooden post
my hammock swings in the generous host
of the shade of late afternoon
I lie here in the cooling breeze
and through the slits of lazy eyes
the undulating meadow flows
to the distant maple row

I am dozing but not long
Comes the pad of bare feet among
the ferns by the pebbled path
It is the children from their nap
Heidi and Bronwen tumble in with me
their bare fat bodies still warm from sleep
They wiggle and giggle and say
Let's go to England Papa today

One shove of the foot against the elm root
and we're off for old England in a cloth boat
sailing over the children's sea
so green with lush clover and tall timothy

ARAN KNIT

The men of Ouratagapple
are cable stitched to the wall
in the pub at Oatquarter
large hands wrapped around
rudders of Guinness

They murmur like low tide
on the strand below Kilmurvey

The lamp flickers like a cuckoo

When time is called
they unravel slowly

Cigarettes hiss under
visored caps

I'LL BET

I'll bet
there is a place
where cows
eat in New York
come home
through Vermont
and are milked
in Massachusetts

NEAR ENNIS

A farmer is returning
from the creamery
wearing rubber knee boots
black trousers
muddy suit coat

He straddles the wagon bed
reins in hand
horse at full gallop
on the road to Lisdoonvarna
green teeth of rain
combing his hair

ON THE EDGE OF THE BURREN

Houses are in hollows
blue gentians
in fissures and sworls

A ruined castle
ivy green
a mile away

The sky is low
eye level
along a blue and white plate

A swan takes off
from the Moyree River
skimming a holly thicket
sounding like a
make and break engine.

PEAT SMOKE

Someone is burning tweed

A mist of Guinness hovers
    over the town

If anyone let their fire out
    there would be a hole
    in the sky

HOW MY GERMAN ANCESTORS CELEBRATED
THE WINTER SOLSTICE

They had this Hessen hillside
maybe foty percent grade
clear cut for a pasture
flanked on both sides
by a dark forest
small castle at the top
where the local lord
could view his holdings
down to the River Weser

Around midnight say
men and boys
dressed sort of like them guys
in those Breughel paintings
wearing that jock strap kind of pouch
over their britches
feathers in their caps
ragged teeth like fangs
probably had a brandy with an egg
would scurry forth
from their thatched homes
go to secret stashes
under sheds and cribs
bringing forth
old wagon wheels
saved all year

stuffed dry straw
between the spokes
set them afire
sent them rolling downhill
while one of the men
blew on a long brass horn

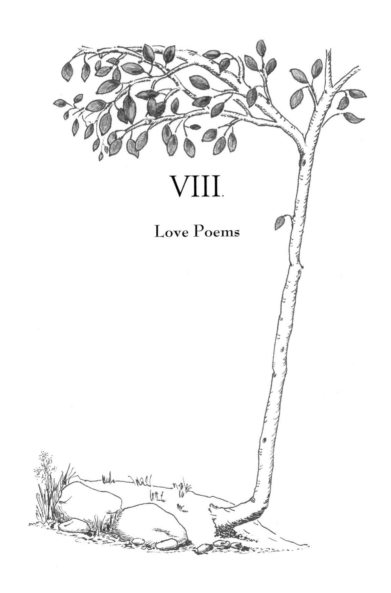

VIII.

Love Poems

IF I AM DREAMING

If I am dreaming
when I die
does the dream go on

Fingernails grow
hair grows
do dreams keep going

If so then I hope
I am dreaming of you
with a gardenia in your hair

WHITE MOUNTAINS IN JUNE

The weather was uncertain, on the cool side
We had a disagreement about which trail to hike
Without an ah yes or no you hoisted your pack
said *See you* and were out of sight

I took a familiar loop trail
I do not like hiking alone when I should be with you
have to keep my eyes down to watch my step
miss much of the surroundings
Half way round the loop a bridge
spanning a deep cut had rotted out
No way could I get down into that chasm
and climb up the other side
Had to return the way I had come
missing the back side of the same scenery

Coming to the trail end I looked ahead
Saw you coming in the other end from your path of choice
waving your arms shouting something
calling to me to look look up
see the snow on the mountain

RINSE WATER

When I do dishes here at our place in New Hampshire
I usually fill the sink with cold rinse water
then the smaller plastic tub with soap and hot water
Do the wine glasses first so they won't pick up grease
then get on with the rest
And of course wouldn't you know
under the fry pan
is a saucer I cooked oatmeal in that morning
and put to soak
Couldn't pour that into the dish water   would cool it off
Not into the rinse water either   dirty it up
Simple Take it out the door
and heave it into the rose bushes
That's the way we do it in the country

When Alan was staying at his son's home in the city
we took turns sitting with him by his bedside
Could not think that he was dying
Street noise sirens boot heels on the brick sidewalk cars
Alan liked to have classical music playing in the background
I would take a break go down the corridor
into the kitchen at the back of the house
and step out into the cold November night
There was a settee a patch of lawn and lilacs
closed in by a high wooden fence
I stood out there alone let the tears spill

Back inside I would try my hand at a little house keeping
cleaning up the many dishes that accumulated from family
    and keepers
It was a new kitchen to me
took some time to figure out where things went
Fill up the sink with cold water
find and fill a tub with hot water and soap
And there of course under some tinfoil was a casserole dish
    soaking
Same drill out the door and fling the water onto the lawn

YOU SAY

your hair
turns red
after
we make love
I wouldn't know
my eyes
are shut tight
they don't open
til I am on my back
The ceiling
of our bedroom
is filled with
red and blue
shiny stars
the kind
they used to
put on my forehead
when I was
a good boy

BREAKING THE WAVES

Supposing you lose your hearing altogether
I would learn sign language
I would try to speak slower
so's you could read my lips
You could still play yer fiddle
by watching my fingers
you've always been good at that.
We could set you on top of the bass drum
so's you could feel the beat
I would try my best to show you the tune

Should I become completely blind
I hope you would read to me
tell me what the grandkids look like
take me by the arm
help me into the canoe

If it happens that I can no longer make love
would you abstain with me
Or would you find a good man to do it with
telling me later sharing the experience
like the woman in that flic BREAKING THE WAVES

The other day you lost yer glasses
couldn't read yer book
couldn't read yer book on the porch
like you had looked forward to doing
We sat rocking looking out to sea
After a while you went up to take a nap
I took my book out of my pack

WALTZ

Sunday evenings I read
You work at your desk by the stove
Telemann's STRING CONCERTOS
filling the room

The Divertimento in three-quarter time
gets me out of my seat
to tap you on the shoulder

You put down pen and glasses
to waltz with me around the room
both in our slippers

Sometimes you put your
face on my shoulder
and after I find a wet spot there

Today after the dance around
I am taking a nap
while the music goes on

I have forgotten there is
another piece in waltz time

I am deep in sleep
but the music comes through

I imagine you
sometime long away
some snowy Sunday
whirling around the room
arms hugging the air

WIDOW

A Love Poem

She rises before daylight
goes out to the main room
still warm from day before
puts a stick in the stove
plays with the cats
cooks some oatmeal
the dark and the warmth comfort her

She is familiar with that comfort
sits at her computer
checking the emails
as the harsh winter sun
glows in the east.

Perhaps one of her children
will drop by later

NEWS

The bad news is
if you die before your wife does
she probably will have an affair
sooner or later

The good news is
you will know about it
& it will be like you are doing it

The bad news is
your wife won't know it's you

The good news is
the other guy won't know either
but he will know you were better

More News

The bad news is
if your wife dies before you do
you will probably have an affair
sooner or later
but you will spend most of that time
looking for someone like your wife

The good news is
your wife will know this

The bad news is
whoever you find
will not be like your wife
even though you wish she were

The good news is
your wife will know this too

LOVE POEM

Being as how
I am the world's worst carpenter
I can roll a marble
from one end of the floor
to the other
Soup dribbles off the
south end of the bowl
The lower end of the house
is really the lower end

I put down a granite slab
to set the stove on
It stays put
even heaves up a few inches
from the frost
while the floor settles around it

You stand on the granite
a statuesque woman
I stand below you on the floor
We are face to face
nipple to nipple

HE HOPES

that the day of
his memorial service
is sort of on the
coolish side
sunny
windy
scarf tossing

that the swelling
organ and trumpet
have filled
eyes and stone

that someone read
Hardy's GREAT THINGS

that there will be dancing
and you are able to
smile and dance

And after outside
friends gather
in circles
around you

then you get
into a car
to go where

DIRECTIONS

There have been
many discussions
on the best way
to get to Alewife.
I favor Routes 3 and 2
being as how
that is the way I know
and besides it
has that great
view of Boston
as you come down the hill
on the Arlington Belmont line
and it goes by the pond
where I grew up
can see my old house from there

You prefer Route 93
no construction going on
and make your way cross lots
through stop lights
along the Mystic River
This is your way
You pore over maps
plot the short cuts
figuring the best way
These are roads that
you may travel alone one day
You have to get used to them.

THE EMPTY NEST

The empty nest
makes it possible for me
to walk naked through the house
at any time
but for you to see me
in this attire
must only serve to
bring to bear
that I am able to be
in this state of undress
because your bird has flown

ESCAPE

After visiting his mom in the nursing home
upon leaving he would
pass by the nurses' station saying
I am escaping   where's the door
and they would chuckle
open the door for him
Now he is a resident
at the very same home
has his knapsack for sweater and book
belly pack for water
walking stick and good boots
shuffle by the station saying
I'm escaping   heh   heh
and they unlock the door
He heads for the gazebo
where his mom used to sit
to read watch the birds
look at the flowers
He sits and pretends to read
but actually he is planning his escape
saving his strength day by day
will need stash of food
from dinner the night before
apple from breakfast
go by the desk saying *I'm gone*
cuppa cawfee at the shop
stash the donut

bye to the boys
I'm escaping   yeah we know
and off to the gazebo
through the hole in the fence there
disappear into the woods
he knows the path to the dirt road
the logging road
the way to his house
He goes over the plan every day
and you know he is coming
have set the table
poured the wine
ALBIONI CONCERTO on
made up the bed

BEDROOM

Not used much daytimes
accept to change clothes going out
or get laundry ready
mostly just for sleeping
No heat like it cold
Sun pours in
south and west windows
looks out on fields
through some spruces to garden
distant valley and hills
all deeply wooded
Pine paneled bare walls
knots with shapes of tornados
or water spouts with reflections
no pictures or book shelves

When I get old
I will spend more time there
install a small heater
cd player
Sit in bed propped up
read   listen to Vivaldi
watch the cats in the garden
birds in the spruces and honeysuckle
Have paintings on the wall
Breughel   Paquin   a calendar
Go out to the kitchen

about as often as I used to
use the bedroom
maybe have a sherry
smell the woodsmoke
go back to bed

BRINGING IN WOOD

Having pulled a muscle
in my back
I lie flat on the couch
ice on my bum
like an old man
unable to work

Jacqueline will not
let me bring in the wood
for the stove

She steps out alone
into the cold
wearing my red and black
wood-carrying-in shirt

GOING FOR A WALK

side by side
with me sometimes getting ahead
then turning
waiting for you to catch up
Now you get ahead of me
and wait

You like to walk at noon
when the sun is strong
You go alone these days
the same route
I know your way by heart
Through the village
down the hill by the pond
hi to the swan hi to the beavers
up the hill through a wood
across the field to home

I like to walk late in the afternoon
when the day has quieted down
I trod a different path
I must leave a note
to tell you where I am going

WHATEVER WORKS

A Love Poem

> *HE: I Can't think of a one..*
> *SHE: Neither can I..*

—Old Joke

It wasn't his wife's fault that he couldn't climax
Doctor said Try fantasy
So his wife became redheads blondes
big tits small tits tall fat
In all manner of places
hotels motels cars front seat and back
busses planes trains

Then he imagined she was herself
and *he* was someone else
in a new bevy of bedrooms

Then he cooked up a scene
where *she* was imagining *him* as someone else
and he wondered if *he* was the same guy
he imagined himself being

And then there was the one where he imagined that
she was imagining *she* was someone else
doing it with *him*
and he wondered if she thought she was a redhead

Sometimes he is himself and she's being herself
and they're on their first date
swimming ballicky
and go at it on the pine needles
It's the best

SONNET FOR JACQUELINE

The night we danced our first real dance together
was cold—February wind and snow
Your legs were bare unmindful of the weather
Now you say *No way I wore red hose*

But I remember pale white legs   Never
thought cold bothered you   Now I picture
you standing among the summer flowers
absorbing heat storing up for winter

You eyes sparkle still   your hair is gray
I am sorry I helped to make it so
Your hair curls around your ears and face
I wish that I could drive away the cold

The weather channel says there is a storm
I will do my best to keep you warm

AFTER

he has gone she says
I'll not play the fiddle for
square dances without him
she says I can't bear to think of
going out the door alone
fiddle on shoulder no way
I'll find something else to do
Yet here she is
striding down the street
fiddle on her back
in high heel boots
black jeans tee shirt
from some festival
gray hair curling
around her ears pretty

GAME

Salt water hoves into view
and she is outa the car shouting
I'm gonna touch it first
kicking off one sandal
then the other
and away she goes
over the rocks
I tie my boots
get my walking stick
follow right behind
but she is already there
arms raised in victory
The slabs are slippery
I look up see her
coming towards me
arms out
hands cupped
like a small bowl
saying *Touch it*
taste it

PASS THE STICK

Pass the stick from me to you
Pass the stick and do just like I do

—Old Game

for Jacqueline

The place we're talking about
is ten miles off the coast
out of the country
No trees there
maybe some scrub alders
Found this stick
in the seaweed low tide
end curved just right for the hand
Peeled some of the bark
let it dry out
Stays with me
all the time on island
You and I
poke around tidal pools
clamber over rocks
At night walk the trail
at the sea edge
see the lights of America
across the bay
Before we go off island
in the fall
I hide the stick

never mind where
tell you later sometime
It will change to a snake
if anyone else finds it
It spends the winter
sheltered from storms
waiting for spring
knowing I will come back
or you
or the children
or their kids

SALT

She heads for the sea
whenever she can
says if it doesn't numb the ankles
ok with her even October

Like a dolphin into the breakers

After catch her looking beachward
like a seal see if I am watching

Won't take a shower for days
fear of losing the salt on her skin
She's a walking salt lick

Inland she works up a sweat
splitting wood weeding
gets her fix like that

Sometimes I cause her to cry
not on purpose mind you
but she is sad that I barely
stay in the water
want to shower after

Sort of like salt in the wounds
I like salt too
would suck all her tears dry
but I leave them for her

HOW TO BECOME A SWAN

She already has
the white throat
& thrusting breast
stroke
eats lots of greens
She spends
evenings on the shore
coaxing the lone swan
to come on land
eat from her hand
learning the song

EQUATION

He wants to
but doesn't
want her to

she wants to
but doesn't
want him to

so there they sit
in parentheses
and kisses

going into
each other but
not into others

and that's the way
it goes with
some odd numbers

IN QUEBEC

You asked about that poem
where I am pitching hay
with some lads in Canada
and I tell you that I almost
inherited a working farm
in Ulverton Quebec

Thirty head of purebred Milking Shorthorns
some sheep and two teams of draft horses
hundred acres of rolling pasture
hayland and maple grove
down to the St Francis River

How come you didn't take it you asked

*Well I was only sixteen at the time
Didn't want to change citizenship
Besides there was plenty of
hockey*
         *square dancing and farming
ten miles from downtown Boston then
Little did I know*
                    *But if I had taken it
                    I wouldn't have met you*

And you replied *I would have found you*

ABOUT THE AUTHOR

Dudley Laufman was raised in the Boston area but has lived most of his adult years in New Hampshire. He lives on the edge of the woods in Canterbury with Jacqueline.

Since 1986, Jacqueline and Dudley Laufman have been playing for dances as *Two Fiddles*. Prior to that, Dudley, who has been playing and calling dances for sixty years, has been the leader of Canterbury Country Dance Orchestra, the first dance band to make an LP recording of the New England jigs and reels most often used for dancing.

photo by Ken Williams

Jacqueline and Dudley have an earthy sound that combines with the beating of their feet as they call out the figures for old time New Hampshire barn and square dances. They are self-taught and play by ear, having learned by the oral tradition.

Dudley has been nominated for a Pushcart Award and is the recipient of the Governor's Award in the Arts Lifetime Achievement Folk Heritage Award for 2001. He has also been nominated for a National Heritage Fellowship and is featured in two films , THE OTHER WAY BACK and COUNTRY CORNERS.